P9-DGU-220

And the Green Grass Grew All Around

ALSO BY ALVIN SCHWARTZ

Chin Music
Tall Talk and Other Talk

Cross Your Fingers, Spit in Your Hat
Superstitions and Other Beliefs

Flapdoodle
Pure Nonsense from American Folklore

Kickle Snifters and Other Fearsome Critters

More Scary Stories to Tell in the Dark

Scary Stories 3
More Tales to Chill Your Bones

Scary Stories to Tell in the Dark

Telling Fortunes
Love Magic, Dream Signs, and Other Ways to Learn the Future

Tomfoolery
Trickery and Foolery with Words

A Twister of Twists, a Tangler of Tongues

Unriddling
All Sorts of Riddles to Puzzle Your Guessery,
Collected from American Folklore

When I Grew Up Long Ago
Older People Talk About the Days When They Were Young

Whoppers
Tall Tales and Other Lies

Witcracks
Jokes and Jests from American Folklore

And the Green Grass Grew All Around

FOLK POETRY FROM EVERYONE

Alvin Schwartz

ℰ ILLUSTRATIONS BY SUE TRUESDELL ℰ

HarperCollins*Publishers*

WITHDRAWAL

11 Winchester Street
Warrenton, VA 22186

"Teddy Bear, Teddy Bear went to a party," on page 100, is reprinted from "Some Rope-Jumping Rhymes from Berkeley, 1943," pp. 278–79, by Mimi Clair, *Western Folklore,* v. 13, by permission of the California Folklore Society.

AND THE GREEN GRASS GREW ALL AROUND: *Folk Poetry from Everyone*
Text copyright © 1992 by Alvin Schwartz
Illustrations copyright © 1992 by Susan G. Truesdell
Printed in the U.S.A.
All rights reserved.

Library of Congress Cataloging-in-Publication Data
Schwartz, Alvin, date
    And the green grass grew all around : folk poetry from everyone /
by Alvin Schwartz ; illustrated by Sue Truesdell.
        p.   cm.
    Includes bibliographical references.
    ISBN 0-06-022757-5.—ISBN 0-06-022758-3 (lib. bdg.)
    1. Folk poetry, American.   I. Title
PS477.S39   1992   89-26722
398.2'0973—dc20   CIP
                                                                       AC

Typography by David Saylor
2 3 4 5 6 7 8 9 10

For
Barbara and Ellie,
John, Peter, Liz,
and Daniel,
Nancy, Betsy, and Walter,
and Susannah

❧ Contents ❧

"Skinny bone, skinny bone . . ."

My first week in school, I was so scared I burst into tears, and somebody started chanting,

> *"Cry, baby, cry,*
> *Stick your finger in your eye,*
> *Tell your mother it wasn't I."*

When others joined in, it didn't help.

I was not only scared that first year, I was skinny. And I soon learned there was a rhyme for that as well. It went:

> *Skinny bone, skinny bone,*
> *In the corner all alone.*

I heard *that* again and again.

In the years that followed, I learned hundreds of rhymes from other children. Some we chanted, others we sang. We used them in games and to be silly. We used them to make fun of how grown-ups behaved and to show our feelings about people we liked and didn't like. We even had rhymes about what was going on in the world, about politics, strikes, dictators and war. And we had rhymes to make our wishes come true.

I knew many rhymes before I went to school. Most of these were nursery rhymes I learned from my parents. They were fun, but they were not as important to me as the ones I learned from other children.

I never thought about who made up this poetry I used. I just took it for granted that other children had done so. For the most part I was right. But I learned later, in writing this book, that some of them had lived many years before I was born.

I also learned that some of "my" rhymes actually were bits and pieces of songs people once sang and that others were "take-offs" on hymns and carols. And I found that some were very old, like counting-out rhymes. "Eena" and "meena," it turned out, were not just silly words, but numbers shepherds had used to count their sheep thousands of years before.

Then I learned one other thing. Children all over the world had rhymes like mine with the same ideas and the same rhythms. But this was not too surprising, for children everywhere are pretty much the same.

When I finished with school, this poetry did not stop. I heard riddles in rhyme and weather predictions and ways to tell the future. And I heard poems about love, work, crime, death and other serious matters. There even were long stories in rhyme that people had made up and recited or sang.

This book is my personal record of such "folk poetry." It is called that because ordinary people made it up in their everyday language to meet their everyday needs. Such poets are called "folk poets." Since their poetry usually is not written down, just passed from one person to another, no one knows who most of these folk poets are. Maybe you are one.

There are about three hundred poems here that are my favorites. They are funny, silly, scary, sad and useful, and a few are beautiful. There are, of course, thousands more to choose from, and they are everywhere.

ALVIN SCHWARTZ

ix

And the
Green Grass Grew
All Around

I. People

The poems in this chapter are about you and me: how we look, how we behave, how silly and sweet we can be.

Fudge, fudge, tell the judge,
Mama's had a baby! . . .

First a daughter, then a son,
And the world is well begun.

First a son, then a daughter,
You've begun as you oughter.

Fudge, fudge, tell the judge
Mama's had a baby!
It's a boy, full of joy,
Papa's going crazy!
How many kisses did he give it?
1, 2, 3, 4, 5 . . .*

I was my mother's darling child
Brought up with care and trouble.
For fear a spoon would hurt my mouth,
She fed me with a shovel.

*This is a jump-rope rhyme. You count each jump until you miss, and
that's how many kisses Papa gave the baby.

Oh, policeman, policeman,
Don't take me,
I've got a wife and a family.
How many children have you got?
Twenty-five, and that's a lot.

Down by the ocean, down by the sea,
Johnny broke a bottle
And blamed it on me.
I told Ma, Ma told Pa,
Johnny got a lickin',
Ha, ha, ha!

My father is a butcher,
My mother cuts the meat,
I'm the little meatball
That runs down the street.

3

My mother, your mother
Live across the way,
Every night they have a fight
And this is what they say,
Acabaca soda cracker, acabaca boo,
Acabaca soda cracker, OUT goes you.

Katalena Magdalena Hoopensteiner Walla Walla Hogan
    Bogan
Is my name.
It *is* a funny name,
But my parents gave it to me
Just the same, same, same. . . .

4

My name is Yon Yonson,
I come from Visconsin,
I verk in der lumberyard dere.
Ven I come down de street
All de people I meet say,
"Vat's your name?"
Und I say,
"My name is Yon Yonson,
I come from Visconsin,
I verk in der lumberyard dere. . . ."

On the mountain is a woman,
But who she is I do not know.
On her head are golden ribbons
And her hair is white as snow.

5

Do your ears hang low,
Do they wobble to and fro?
Can you tie them in a knot,
Can you tie them in a bow?
Can you throw them over your shoulder
Like a Continental soldier?
Can you pluck a merry tune?
Do your ears hang low?

Tune: *Turkey in the Straw*

Do your ears hang low, Do they wob-ble to and fro? Can you
tie them in a knot, — Can you tie them in a bow?

When God gave out noses,
I thought He said "roses,"
So I asked for a big red one.
When He handed out legs,
I thought He said "kegs,"
So I asked for two big round ones.

When He gave out looks,
I thought He said "books,"
So I said I didn't want any.
When He handed out brains,
I thought He said "trains,"
And I missed mine.

I would reduce,
But what's the use?
The bigger the berry,
The sweeter the juice.

Jerry Hall
Is so small,
A mouse could eat him
Hat and all.

Little dabs of powder,
Little dabs of paint
Make a girl look
Like she ain't.

After the ball was over,
She lay on the sofa and sighed.
She put her false teeth in salt water
And took out her lovely glass eye.
She kicked her wood leg in the corner,
Hung up her wig on the wall,
She closed her real eye and sang softly
"After the Ball."

Tune: *After the Ball*

Af - ter the ball was o - ver, She

lay on the so - fa and sighed. _____ She

put her false teeth in salt wa - ter And

took out her love - ly glass eye. _____

I with I wath a fith,
I with I wath a fith,
I'd thwim and thwim the deep blue thea,
I with I wath a fith.

I with I wath a thip,
I with I wath a thip,
I'd thail and thail the deep blue thea,
I with I wath a thip.

I with I wath a thafety pin,
I with I wath a thafety pin,
I'd rutht and rutht till everything butht,
I with I wath a thafety pin.

I with I wath thum thlime,
I with I wath thum thlime,
I'd ooth and ooth in everyone's thoose,
I with I wath thum thlime.

I with I wathn't a thimp,
I with I wathn't a thimp,
I'd thing a thong that had thum thenthe,
I with I wathn't a thimp.

Tune: *The Farmer in the Dell*

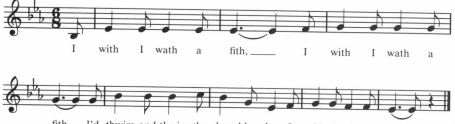

I with I wath a fith, ___ I with I wath a

fith, _ I'd thwim and thwim the deep blue thea, I with I wath a fith. _

Violetta is in the pantry
Gnawing on a bone,
How she gnaws it,
How she claws it
When she thinks she is alone.

II

Gene, Gene, made a machine,
Frank, Frank, turned the crank,
Joe, Joe, made it go,
Art, Art, lit the spark
And blew it all apart.

Anna Elise, she jumped with surprise.
The surprise was so quick,
It played her a trick.
The trick was so rare,
She jumped in a chair.
The chair was so frail,
She jumped in a pail.
The pail was so wet,
She jumped in a net.
The net was so small,
She jumped on a ball.
The ball was so round,
She jumped on the ground.
And ever since then
She's been turning around.

There was a fellow,
His name was Jack,
He tried to get to Heaven
In a Cadillac.
The Cadillac broke,
Down he fell,
Instead of Heaven,
He went to—
Now don't get excited,
Don't lose your head,
Instead of Heaven,
He went to bed.

There was a girl named Mary Lou
Who one day had nothing to do.
She sat on the stairs
And counted her hairs,
Ninety-four thousand three hundred and two.

Tell me quick before I faint,
Is we friends, or is we ain't?

The grapes hang green upon the vine,
I chose you as a friend of mine.
I chose you out of all the rest—
The reason is I love you best.

❧ 2. Food ❧

Some folk poets think that eating
is the most delicious thing they do
and also the funniest.

Here I stand all fat and chunky,
Ate a duck and swallowed a donkey.

Ravioli, ravioli—
Ravioli, that's the stuff for me.
Do you have it on your sleeve?
Yes, I have it on my sleeve.
On your sleeve?
On my sleeve.
Ravioli, ravioli—
Ravioli, that's the stuff for me.

Do you have it on your pants?
Yes, I have it on my pants.
On your pants?
On my pants.
On your sleeve?
On my sleeve.
Ravioli, ravioli—
Ravioli, that's the stuff for me.

Do you have it on your shoe?
Yes, I have it on my shoe.
On your shoe?
On my shoe.
On your pants?
On my pants.
On your sleeve?
On my sleeve.
Ravioli, ravioli—
Ravioli, that's the stuff for me.

The singers add as many articles of clothing as they can think of.

Tune: *Alouette*

Ra - vi - o - li, ra - vi - o - li, ra - vi - o li, that's the stuff for me.

Do you have it on your sleeve? Yes, I have it on my sleeve. On my sleeve, on my sleeve.

On top of spaghetti
All covered with cheese,
I lost my poor meatball
When somebody sneezed.

It rolled off the table
And onto the floor,
Then my poor meatball
Rolled out the door.

It rolled into the garden
And under a bush,
And then my poor meatball
Was nothing but mush.

But the mush was so tasty,
As tasty can be,
Early last summer
It grew into a tree.

The tree was all covered
With beautiful moss
And grew lots of meatballs
In to-mato sauce.

So when you eat spaghetti
All covered with cheese,
Hang on to your meatball
And don't ever sneeze.

Tune: *On Top of Old Smoky*

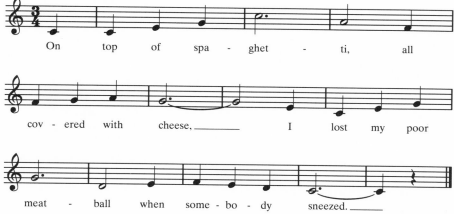

On top of spa - ghet - ti, all

cov - ered with cheese, _____ I lost my poor

meat - ball when some - bo - dy sneezed. _____

Tomatoes, lettuce,
Carrots and peas,
Your mother says
Eat a lot of these.

I eat my peas with honey,
I've done it all my life.
It makes the peas taste funny,
But it keeps them on my knife.

Mary had a little lamb,
A little pork, a little ham,
A little egg, a little toast,
Some pickles and a great big roast,
A lobster and some prunes,
A glass of milk, some macaroons.
It made the waiters grin
To see her order so,
And when they carried Mary out
Her face was white as snow.

Tune: *John Brown's Body*

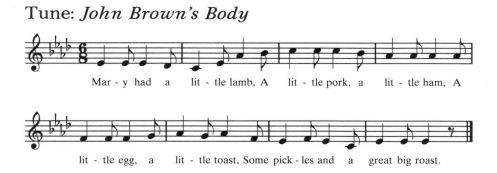

Mar - y had a   lit - tle lamb, A   lit - tle pork, a   lit - tle ham, A

lit - tle egg, a   lit - tle toast, Some pick - les and a   great big roast.

Then there is this version:

Mary ate some marmalade,
And Mary ate some jam,
Mary ate some oyster sauce,
And Mary ate some ham,
Mary drank some lemonade
And also ginger beer,
And Mary wondered what it was
That made her feel so queer.

Whoops came the marmalade,
And whoops came the jam,
Whoops came the oyster sauce,
And whoops came the ham,
Whoops came the lemonade
And the ginger beer,
And Mary knew what it was
That made her feel so queer.

When I found a mouse in my stew,
I raised a great hullabaloo.
"Please don't shout," the waiter said,
"Or the rest will want one too."

Oh my,
I want a piece of pie.
The pie's too sweet,
I want a piece of meat.
The meat's too red,
I want a piece of bread.
The bread's too brown,
I'd better go to town.
Town's too far,
I need a trolley car.
The car's too slow,
I fell and stubbed my toe.
My toe's got a pain,
I'd better take a train.
The train had a wreck,
I nearly broke my neck.
Oh, my, no more pie.

22

Some gum, chum?

I scream,
You scream,
We all scream
For ice cream.

Through the teeth,
Past the gums,
Look out stomach,
Here it comes!

Better to urp a burp
And bear the shame
Than squelch a belch
And die of pain.

Now I lay me down to sleep,
A bag of peanuts at my feet,
If I die before I wake,
I must have died of a bellyache.

Just plant a watermelon on my grave
And let the juice seep through *(slurp!)*,
Just plant a watermelon on my grave,
That's all I ask of you.

Now southern fried chicken tastes mighty fine,
But all I want is a watermelon vine,
So plant a watermelon on my grave
And let the juice seep through *(slurp!)*.

❧ 3. School ❧

If you haven't found out yet,
school is *not* a perfect place.

Row, row, row your boat
Gently down the stream,
Throw your teacher overboard
And you will hear her scream.

Heigh-ho, heigh-ho,
It's off to school we go,
The teachers look like Frankenstein,
The water tastes like turpentine,
Heigh-ho, heigh-ho.

Tune: *Heigh-Ho, Heigh-Ho*

Running to school,
Can't be late,
Gotta be there
By half-past eight.

Here comes teacher with a great big stick,
Wonder how I did in arithmetic.

Here comes teacher, and she is yellin',
Wonder how I did when it came to spellin'.

I've been working on my schoolbooks
All the livelong day,
I've been working on my schoolbooks
Just to pass.

Tune: *I've Been Working on the Railroad*

I've been work-ing on my school-books all the live-long day,

I've been work-ing on my school-books just to pass.

Teacher's pet, teacher's pet,
Never missed a lesson yet.

Mary had a stick of gum,
She chewed it long and slow,
And everywhere that Mary went
That gum was sure to go.
It followed her to school one day
Which was against the rule,
And the teacher took the gum away
And chewed it after school.

Tune: *John Brown's Body*

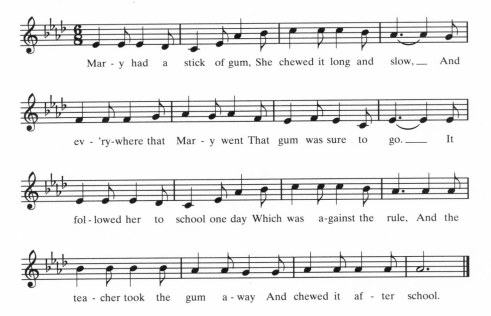

Mar - y had a stick of gum, She chewed it long and slow, __ And

ev - 'ry-where that Mar - y went That gum was sure to go. __ It

fol - lowed her to school one day Which was a-gainst the rule, And the

tea - cher took the gum a - way And chewed it af - ter school.

Naughty little Margaret
Scribbles in her books,
Doesn't do her lessons,
But cares about her looks.
When the teacher hollers,
"What is that awful noise?"—
Why, it's naughty little Margaret
Kissing all the boys.

Heigh-ho, heigh-ho,
I bit the teacher's toe,
The dirty rat, she bit me back,
Heigh-ho, heigh-ho.

Tune: *Heigh-Ho, Heigh-Ho*

On top of Old Smoky,
All covered with sand,
I shot my poor teacher
With a green rubber band.
I shot her with pleasure,
I shot her with pride,
I could not have missed her,
She's forty feet wide.

Tune: *On Top of Old Smoky*

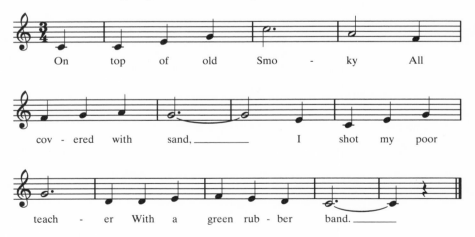

On top of old Smo - ky All

cov - ered with sand, _____ I shot my poor

teach - er With a green rub - ber band. _____

Mine eyes have seen the glory
Of the closing of the school.
We have tortured all the teachers,
We have broken every rule.
We plan to hang the principal
Tomorrow afternoon,
Our truth is marching on.
Glory, glory hallelujah,
Glory, glory hallelujah,
Our truth is marching on.

Tune: *Battle Hymn of the Republic*

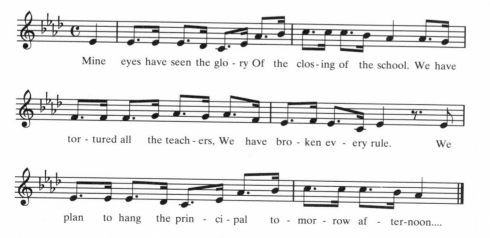

Mine eyes have seen the glo - ry Of the clos - ing of the school. We have

tor - tured all the teach - ers, We have bro - ken ev - ery rule. We

plan to hang the prin - ci - pal to - mor - row af - ter-noon....

If I had you for a teacher,
I'd be a happy creature.

Hark, the herald angels shout,
One more day and we get out,
One more day till we are free
From this penitentiary.

Tune: *Hark, the Herald Angels Sing*

Hark,   the   her - ald   an - gels   shout, _____

One   more   day   and   we   get   out....

No more pencils, no more books,
No more teachers' dirty looks,
No more things that bring us sorrow,
For we won't be here come tomorrow.

⚜ 4. Teases and Taunts ⚜

If somebody makes you mad, there are thirty-one
rhymes here to help you say what you think.

Don't say it, don't say it!
Your mother will faint,
Your father will fall
In a bucket of paint.

Baby, baby,
Suck your thumb,
Wash your hair
In bubble gum.

Cry, baby, cry,
Stick your finger in your eye,
Tell your mother it wasn't I.

Cowardy, cowardy custard,
Eat your father's mustard.

Liar, liar, pants on fire,
Tongue as long as a telephone wire.

Cross my heart and hope to die,
Cut me in half if I told a lie.

Shame, shame,
Everybody knows your name.

There is a girl on our street
Who is very deceitful,
Every little tittle-tat
She goes and tells the people,
Big nose, funny face,
Put her in a glass case.
———————— is her name.

Tattletale, tattletale,
Place your britches on a nail,
Hang them high, hang them low,
Hang them in a picture show.

Stare, stare like a bear
Sitting in your underwear.

Fat, fat, the water rat,
Fifty bullets in his hat.

Skinny bone, skinny bone,
In the corner all alone.

Roses are red,
Cabbages are green,
You have a shape
Like a washing machine.

Roses are red,
Violets are black,
Do me a favor,
Go sit on a tack.

Roses are red,
Violets are blue,
A face like yours
Belongs in the zoo.

*These rhymes grew from this one written four hundred
years ago:*

> Roses are red, violets are blue,
> All the sweetest flowers in the forest grew.

*The English poet Edmund Spenser wrote it as part of his
famous poem* The Faerie Queene.

I love you, I love you,
I love you, I do.
But don't get excited,
I love monkeys, too.

Mind your own business,
Fry your own fish,
But don't poke your nose
Into my dish.

Too bad,
So sad,
You're mad,
I'm glad.

I'm the boss, Applesauce.

No way, José.

Jane, Jane, the windowpane.

Willie, Willie wheezer,
Pigtail squeezer.

Robert, Bedobert, Hadobert, Gofobert,
High-legged, two-legged, bow-legged Robert.

Susie, Susie Sauerkraut,
Does your mother know you're out?

There she goes, there she goes,
All dressed up in her Sunday clothes,
Ain't she sweet, ain't she sweet?
All but the smell of her dirty feet.

Tune: *The Hearse Song*

There she goes, _____ There she goes, _____

All dressed up in her Sun - day clothes....

Twinkle, twinkle, little star,
What you say is what you are.

Tune: *Twinkle, Twinkle, Little Star*

Twin-kle, twin-kle, lit - tle star, What you say is what you are.

Silence in the court,
The monkey wants to speak,
No laughing or talking
Or stamping your feet.

You call me names?
My strength you doubt?
Pardon me
While I knock you out.

See my pinky?
See my thumb?
See my fist?
You'd better run.

Sticks and stones will break my bones,
But names will never hurt me,
And when you're dead and in your grave,
You'll pay for what you called me.

Understand, rubber band?

5. Wishes—and Warnings

There are rhymes here that tell the future
and others that make your wishes come true.
Some say it is the sound of the words rhyming
that gives these poems their magic.

Needles, pins,
Triplets, twins . . .

If your shoelace comes untied,
It is a sign sure and true,
That at that very moment
Your love thinks of you.

Step on a spoon,
You'll be married soon.

Step on a knife,
You'll lead a lonely life.

If your nose itches,
Someone is coming
With a hole
In his britches.

42

If you sneeze:

Once, a wish,
Twice, a kiss,
Three times, a letter,
Four times, something better.

See a pin
And pick it up,
All day long
You'll have good luck.

See a pin
And let it lay,
Bad luck you'll have
All the day.

Count the birds in a tree:

One for anger,
Two for mirth,
Three for a wedding,
Four for a birth,
Five for rich,
Six for poor,
Seven for a witch,
I can tell you no more.
Birds, birds, chatter and flee,
Turn up your tails,
And good luck to thee.

Fortune-teller, fortune-teller,
Please tell me
What am I going to be:
Butcher, baker, undertaker,
Tinker, tailor, bow-legged sailor,
Rich man, poor man, beggar man, thief,
Doctor, lawyer, merchant, chief.

*Recite this as you skip rope. When you miss, you will have
the answer.*

*If you and a friend say the same word at the same time,
make a wish. Then link your left pinkies and say:*

Needles, pins,
Triplets, twins,
When a man marries
His trouble begins.
When a man dies,
His trouble ends.
What goes up a chimney?
Smoke.
May your wish and mine
Never be broke.

45

I wish I were a dancer
I wish I were a star,
I wish I had a beautiful
Big red car.

Touch blue,
Your wish will come true.

6. Love and Marriage

Does he love me? Will she marry me? Folk poets seem more interested in this subject than any other.

Somebody loves you
Deep and true.
If I weren't so shy,
I'd tell you who.

He is handsome,
He is pretty,
He is a boy from the city.
One, two, three,
Oh, please tell me,
Who is he?

Down by the river where the green grass grows
There sat Mary sweet as a rose,
Along came Johnny and kissed her on the nose.
How many kisses did she get?
1, 2, 3 . . .

Beneath a shady tree they sat,
He held her hand, she held his hat,
I held my breath and lay quite flat.
They kissed—I saw them do it.

He said that kissing was no crime,
She held her face up every time,
I held my breath and wrote this rhyme,
And they never knew I knew it.

Some kiss behind a lily,
Some kiss behind a rose,
But the proper place to kiss
Is *underneath* the nose.

I never saw such eyes as thine,
If you'll butcher hand in mine,
I'll liver around you every day
And seek for us a ham-let far away.

Two on a hammock
Ready to kiss
When all of a sudden
It went like SIHT.

Sister has a boyfriend
Comes every night,
Walks in the parlor
And turns out the light.
I peep through the keyhole,
What do I see?
"Johnny, Johnny, Johnny,
Put your arms around me."

I wish I had a nickel,
I wish I had a dime,
I wish I had a boyfriend
To love me all the time,

I'd make him wash the dishes,
I'd make him wash the floor,
And if he didn't do it,
I'd kick him out the door.

I wish my mother would hold her tongue,
She had a beau when she was young.
I wish my father would do the same,
He met a girl and changed her name.

I love that black-eyed boy,
I love that black-eyed boy,
His eyes are black,
But he'll never come back.
I love that black-eyed boy.

My heart is not a plaything,
My heart is not a toy,
But if I want it broken,
I'll give it to a boy.

Read	see	that	me	but	not	my	got
up	shall	I'll	love	if	me	love	for
and	you	love	you	it	love	for	be
down	and	you	if	is	you	you	shall

Love many, trust few,
Always paddle your own canoe.

As sure as a vine grows round a stump,
You are my darling sugar lump.

As sure as a vine grows round a rafter,
You are the one that I am after.

I love you, I love you,
I love you lots.
My love for you
Would fill all the pots,
Buckets, pitchers, kettles and cans,
The big washtub and both dishpans.

Roses red, violets blue,
Sugar is sweet, but not like you.
The violets fade, the roses fall,
But you get sweeter all in all.

53

Nobody loves me,
Everybody hates me,
I'm going out and eat worms,
Long, skinny, slimy ones,
Big, fat, juicy ones,
Itsy bitsy teeny ones.
See how they wiggle and squirm!
Yum! Yum!

Anna and Frankie went for a ride,
Frankie said, "Will you be my bride?"
"Oh, yes, my darling! Yes, my dear!"
"Then we'll be married in half a year."

54

Here comes the bride,
Big, fat and wide,
See how she wobbles
From side to side.
Here comes the groom
Skinny as a broom,
He'd wobble too
If he had any room.

Tune: *The Wedding March*

Here comes the bride, Big, fat, and wide,

See how she wob - bles From side___ to side.

Sam and Joan sitting in a tree
K-I-S-S-I-N-G.
First came love, then came marriage,
Then came Joan with a baby carriage.

I wish you luck,
I wish you joy,
I wish you first a baby boy.
And when his hair begins to curl,
I wish for you a baby girl.

❧ 7. Work ❧

There is but one poem in this chapter. Some unknown person in Germany brought it to Pennsylvania over a century ago. It tells how a man struggled to build a good life through his hard work.

When I first came to this land,
I was not a wealthy man. . . .

When I first came to this land,
I was not a wealthy man.
I got myself a shack,
And I called that shack "Break my Back,"
And the land was sweet and good,
And I did what I could.

When I first came to this land,
I was not a wealthy man.
I got myself a farm,
And I called that farm "Muscle in My Arm,"
And I called my shack, "Break My Back,"
And the land was sweet and good,
And I did what I could.

When I first came to this land,
I was not a wealthy man.
I got myself a wife,
And I called that wife "Run for Your Life,"
And I called my farm "Muscle in My Arm,"
And I called my shack "Break My Back,"
And the land was sweet and good,
And I did what I could.

When I first came to this land,
I was not a wealthy man.
I got myself a cow,
And I called that cow "No Milk Now,"
And I called my wife "Run for Your Life,"
And I called my farm "Muscle in My Arm,"
And I called my shack "Break My Back,"
And the land was sweet and good,
And I did what I could.

When I first came to this land,
I was not a wealthy man.
I got myself a son,
And I called that son "Lots of Fun,"
And I called my cow "No Milk Now,"
And I called my wife "Run for Your Life,"
And I called my farm "Muscle in My Arm,"
And I called my shack "Break My Back,"
And the land was sweet and good,
And I did what I could.

When I first came to this land,
I was not a wealthy man.
I got myself a tree,
And I called that tree "Family Tree,"
And I called my son "Lots of Fun,"
And I called my wife "Run for Your Life,"
And I called my cow "No Milk Now,"
And I called my farm "Muscle in My Arm,"
And I called my shack "Break My Back,"
And the land was sweet and good,
And I did what I could.

People have written many poems about their work, for it is one of the most important things in their lives. They have told of the struggles, as this poet has done. They have protested low wages and poor working conditions. And they have shared the pleasures. They even have made up poems to help them get their work done. You will find some of these on pages 157 and 158.

8. Stories

Many folk poems actually are brief stories about
the everyday experiences we have. But the poems
in this chapter are about dramatic events:
a holdup, a shipwreck, the ninth inning in a
baseball game, and a pig run wild.

He dropped his shotgun, whipped out his Colts
And blasted at Louie with twin thunderbolts. . . .

"Reach for the Sky!"

Louie Malone yelled, "Reach for the sky!"
But the guard on the stagecoach
was young and spry. . . .
He dropped his shotgun, whipped out his Colts
And blasted at Louie with twin thunderbolts.
Louie was a robber who robbed all alone,
But now things were hot for Louie Malone.
The slugs buzzed around him like bees in a swarm
As the fight for the money got right warm.
When the smoke cleared away, Louie was found
In a puddle of red—dead on the ground.
The guard wasn't even nicked, and it is true to say
That you can't get away with it,
Crime doesn't pay.

The Titanic

When they built the ship *Titanic*
To sail the ocean blue,
They thought they built a ship
That the water would never get through.
But on its maiden voyage,
An iceberg hit that ship,
Oh, it was sad when the great ship went down,
Went down.

It was sad, it was sad,
It was sad when the great ship went down
To the bottom of the—
Husbands and wives,
Little children lost their lives.
It was sad when the great ship went down,
Went down.

They swung the lifeboats out
O'er the dark and stormy sea,
And the band struck up with
"Nearer My God to Thee."
Little children wept and cried
As the waves came o'er the side.
It was sad when the great ship went down,
Went down.

Tune: *The Titanic*

When they built the ship Ti - tan - ic To

sail the o - cean blue, They __ thought they built a

ship That the wa - ter would nev - er get through. But

on its maid - en voy - age, An ice - berg hit that

ship, Oh it was sad __ when the great __ ship went

down. (Went down) It was sad, _____ It was

sad, _____ It was sad when the great _ ship went

down, (to the bot - tom of the sea) Hus - bands and

wives, Lit - tle chil - dren lost their lives. It was

sad _ when the great _ ship went down. (Went down)

The ocean liner S.S. Titanic *sank during the night of April 14, 1912, after crashing into an iceberg in the North Atlantic. More than fifteen hundred of its passengers drowned.*

Two Runs Will Win the Game

A man on third, two batters out,
Two runs will win the game.
If I could hit a home run clout,
Great would be my fame.

I hitched up my pants,
Spit on my hands,
Pulled down my cap
And faced the howling stands.

"Ball three!" the fans yelled with delight.
"Strike two!" the umpire said.
I knocked the next ball out of sight—
Then fell right out of bed.

The Terrible Pig

The pig was first seen by the men at Gillis Mill,
Then it ran past the station on Dismal Hill.
On a spot in the road there are bristles and hair
Where it met head-on with a big black bear.
A bulldog failed to run it down,
Then it broke the back of a bobcat hound.
A rabbit tried it in a race,
But the pig just left him in disgrace.
It crashed right through Herb Whalen's door,

And left Herb's breakfast on the floor.
It ran between poor Herbie's legs,
And Herb fell back in a pail of eggs.
Ace Gliddin saw the pig was running hard
When it circled round
Through Everett Weissfeld's yard.
It ran right through the side of a shack,
And knocked the owner flat on his back . . .
Then it ran down Cary Street,
The rocks and gravel flew from its feet!
" 'Twas a terror to see," said old Charlie Freel.
"Me blood ran cold when I heard him squeal. . . ."

Old Joe Fanjoy with a heavy load
Came staggering out of Wilcox Road,
He saw the pig and dodged and fell,
"God have mercy!" they heard him yell.
Old Uncle Ellery saw Joe fall,
And grabbed his rifle that hung on the wall.
He fired twice when the pig rushed by,
But his hand shook so that he shot too high,
And on and on ran the terrible pig. . . .

On July 18, 1987, The New York Times *reported that a* real *three-hundred-pound pig was on the loose in Rochester, Massachusetts, setting off burglar alarms, breaking doors off hinges, stealing dog food and keeping clear of the police.*

≈ 9. Nonsense ≈

Nonsense is no sense. It is the opposite of common sense.
What makes a nonsense poem fun is the trick it plays.
You expect it to make sense. But it takes you into a world
where almost nothing is the way it should be.

Order in the court,
The judge is eating beans,
His wife is in the bathtub
Counting submarines.

Oh, I had a horse, his name was Bill,
And when he ran, he couldn't stand still.
One day he ran away,
And I ran with him.

He ran so fast he could not stop,
He ran into a barbershop,
And fell exhaustionized with his eyeteeth
In the barber's left shoulder.

Oh, I had a gal, and her name was Daisy,
And when she sang the cat went crazy
With deliriums, Saint Vituses,
And all kinds of cataleptics.

One day she sang about
A man who turned inside out
And jumped into a river bed,
He was so sleepy.

Oh, I went up in a balloon so big,
The people on earth, they looked like a pig,
Like a mice, like a katydid, like flieses,
Like fleases.

The balloon turned over with its bottom side higher,
It fell on the wife of a country squire,
She made a noise like a dog hound, like a whistle,
Like a stick of dynamite.

Oh, what can you do in a case like that?
What can you do but stamp on your hat,
Or your toothbrush, or your eyeglasses,
Or anything else that's helpless.

73

The monkey married the baboon's sister,
Gave her a ring and then he kissed her.
He kissed so hard, he raised a blister,
She set up quite a yell.

The bridesmaid stuck on a piece of plaster,
It stuck so fast, it couldn't stick faster,
It was a sad disaster,
But it soon got well.

Higglety, pigglety, pop,
The dog has eaten the mop,
The pig's in a hurry,
The cat's in a flurry,
Higglety, pigglety, pop!

Looking through the knothole
Of Grandpa's wooden leg,
Why did they put the shore
So near the ocean?
Who cut the sleeves
Out of dear old Daddy's vest?
Oh, we hope that Grandma's tooth
Will soon fit Jenny.
She hasn't any.

Looking out the window,
A second-story window,
I slipped and sprained my eyebrow
On the pavement.
Run get the Listerine,
Sister's got a beau,
But a boy's best friend is his mother.

The horsey stood around
With his feet upon the ground,
Oh, who will wind my wristwatch
When I'm gone?
We feed the baby garlic
So we can find him in the dark,
For a boy's best friend is his mother,
No other.

Oh, the cow kicked Nelly in the belly in the barn,
The cow kicked Nelly in the belly in the barn,
The cow kicked Nelly in the belly in the barn,
But the farmer said it would do no harm.

Second verse, same as the first,
But a little bit louder
And a little bit worse.

Oh, the cow kicked Nelly in the belly in the barn . . .

Tune: *Turkey in the Straw*

Oh, the   cow kicked Nel - ly   in the   bel - ly   in the barn,   The __

cow   kicked   Nel - ly   in   the   bel - ly   in   the   barn....

*Sing the first verse, then shout the second verse and start
over.*

76

A barefoot boy with shoes on
Came shuffling down the street,
His pants were full of pockets,
His shoes were full of feet.

He was born when just a baby,
His mother's pride and joy,
His only sister was a girl,
His brother was a boy.

He never was a triplet,
He never was a twin,
His legs were fastened to his knees
Just above the shin.

His teeth were fastened in his head
Several inches from his shoulder.
When he grew up he became a man
And every day grew older.

"WHO PUT THE OVERALLS IN MRS. MURPHY'S CHOWDER?"
Nobody answered, so then we shouted louder.
"WHO PUT THE OVERALLS
IN MRS. MURPHY'S CHOWDER?"
Nobody answered, so then we shouted louder.

"WHO PUT THE OVERALLS IN MRS. MURPHY'S CHOWDER?"

Nobody answered, so then we shouted louder . . .

Mama, Mama, have you heard,
Pop's gonna buy me a singing bird.
If that singing bird don't sing,
Pop's gonna buy me a diamond ring.

If that diamond ring gets broke,
Pop's gonna buy me a nanny goat.
If that nanny goat runs away,
Pop's gonna spank my boomzeeay.

If my boomzeeay gets sore,
Pop's gonna take me to the shore.
If the shore is far away,
Pop's gonna take me by the train.

If that train runs off the track,
Pop's gonna get his nickel back.
If his nickel's made of lead,
Pop's gonna get a pop on the head.

79

I'm up here in the nuthouse,
My brain is in a rut,
My keeper says I'm crazy,
But he's just off his nut.
I'm just as sane as you are,
And I can prove it too.
When you hear my lullabye,
You'll know I'm not cuckoo.

Oh, I was born one night one morn
When the whistles went TOOT! TOOT!
I can fry a steak or bake a cake
When the mud pies are in bloom.
Do six and six make nine?
Does ice grow on a vine?
Oh, loopity-loop in the noodle soup,
Just give your shoes a shine.

Oh, I cannot tell the truth,
I stole a Baby Ruth,
It's in a tree beneath the sea
Inside a gopher's tooth.
Oh, Easter eggs will wash their legs
And children will have ducks,
I'd rather buy a lemon pie
For forty-seven bucks.

Oh, I'll sue you all for slander,
I'll make you all repent,
How can I be Napoleon
If I'm the President?

Boom, boom, ain't it great to be crazy,
Boom, boom, ain't it great to be crazy,
To be silly and foolish the whole day through,
Boom, boom, ain't it great to be crazy.

A horse and a flea and three blind mice
Sat on a curbstone shooting dice,
The horse said "Oops!" and fell on the flea,
And the flea said, "Whoops, there's a horsey on me!"

Boom, boom, ain't it great to be crazy . . .

Way down south where the bananas grow,
An ant stepped on an elephant's toe,
The elephant cried with tears in his eyes,
"Why don't you pick on someone your size?"

Boom, boom, ain't it great to be crazy . . .

Tune: *Boom, Boom, Ain't It Great to Be Crazy?*

Boom, boom, ain't it great to be cra - zy, Boom,

boom, ain't it great to be cra - zy, To be

sil - ly and fool - ish the whole day through, Boom,

Verse

boom, ain't it great to be cra - zy. A

horse and a flea and the three blind mice

Sat on a curb - stone shoot - ing dice, The

horse said "Oops!" and fell on the flea, And the

flea said, "Whoops, there's a hor - sey on me!"

As I was going out one day,
My head fell off and rolled away,
When I saw that it was gone,
I picked it up and put it on.

❧ 10. Riddles ❧

Why does a riddle rhyme?
Because it is easier to remember that way.

Four stiff-standers,
Four dilly-danders,
Two lookers, two hookers,
Two flip-flops and a wig-wag.
What is it?

1. What is the difference
   Between a dancer and a duck?
   To solve this riddle
   You will need a lot of luck.

2. As I was going to St. Ives,
   I met a man with seven wives,
   Each wife had seven sacks,
   Each sack had seven cats,
   Each cat had seven kits—
   Kits, cats, sacks, and wives,
   How many were going to St. Ives?

3. Round and round the rugged rock
   The ragged rascal ran.
   How many R's are there in that?
   Now tell me if you can.

4. What is it you always see
   In earth, in fire, in smoke, in tea?
   It is in your feet,
   It is in your head,
   You will even find it in your bed.

5. Light as a feather,
   Nothing in it,
   But few can hold it
   For even a minute.

6. Thirty white cows standing in a stall,
    In comes a red cow and licks them all.

7. Feed it,
    It will grow high.
    Give it water,
    It will die.

8. The first letter in my name
    Is in "wizard" and "warlock" and "white,"
    The second is in "shiver" and in "fright,"
    The third is in "broomstick," also in "cat,"
    The fourth in "magic," but not in "rat,"
    The fifth you will find in "high" and in "hood"—
    For I am a creature who does no good.

9. Many eyes,
   Never cries.

10. It stays all year,
    But it leaves in the spring,
    It has a bark,
    But it doesn't sing.

11. It runs all day, but never walks,
    It often murmurs, but never talks,
    It has a bed, but never sleeps,
    It has a mouth, but never eats.

12. Flies forever,
    Rests never.

13. A snow-white bird
    Floats down through the air,
    And on every tree,
    It lights there.

14.   I saw a peacock with a fiery tail
I saw a comet dropping hail
I saw a cloud with ivy all around
I saw an oak creeping on the ground
I saw an ant swallowing up a whale
I saw the sea overflowing with ale
I saw a glass fifteen feet deep
I saw a well filled with tears we weep
I saw red eyes in a flaming fire
I saw a house bigger than the moon and higher
I saw the sun at twelve o'clock at night
I saw a man who also saw that wondrous sight.

*Did this person really see these things? Add the right
punctuation to this riddle, and you will learn what
he did see.*

90

15. In the beginning
    I seem mysterious,
    But in the end
    I am nothing serious.

    And now, sir,
    Your answer.

Answers

Introduction. A cow (legs, teats, eyes, horns, ears, a tail)

1. A dancer goes quick on her legs,
   A duck goes quack on her eggs.

2. One person was going to St. Ives; the others were coming *from* St. Ives.

3. There aren't any R's in "that."

4. The letter "e."

5. A person's breath.

6. Teeth and a tongue.

7. Fire.

8. W-I-T-C-H.

9. A potato.

10. A tree.

11. A stream or a river.

12. The wind.

13. Snow.

14. Add a comma after the fourth word in each line, except the last line.

15. A riddle.

☙ II. Fun and Games ☙

The rhymes in this chapter will help you to do all sorts
of things: choose who is It, jump rope, bounce a ball
and march and cheer. There is one rhyme that
makes it easier to wash dishes. And there is
another that helps you to sound like a fiddle.

One for the money,
Two for the show,
Three to get ready
And four, let's go!

Counting Out and Choosing Up

When I went up the apple tree,
All the apples fell on me,
Bake a pudding, bake a pie,
Did you ever tell a lie?
Yes, you did,
You know you did,
You broke your mother's teapot lid,
L-I-D spells "lid"
And out goes you!

Intie, mintie, tootsie, lala,
Falama, linkie, dinkie, dala,
Falama lee, falama loo,
Out goes you!

Monkey, monkey, bottle of beer,
How many monkeys are there here?
One is far, one is near,
And you are the one
Who is out, my dear.

94

Wire, briar, limberlock,
Three geese in a flock,
One flew east, one flew west,
One flew over the cuckoo's nest.
The clock fell down,
The mouse ran around,
Scared all the people out of town—
And out goes she
With a dirty dishrag
On her knee!

Eeny, meeny, miney, mo,
Crack a feeny, finny, fo,
Um a wootsey, pop a tootsie,
Rick, stick, band, doe.

Yellow cornmeal,
Red tomato,
Sugar cane,
Sweet potato,
Watermelon,
Ripe persimmon—
Little goober peas.
And out goes you!

There are hundreds of these rhymes we use to learn who will be It. Most were made up by boys and girls in the past hundred years or so. But some are very old, for counting out is an ancient ceremony that once was used for far more serious purposes.

It is said that some of the meaningless words in these rhymes come from rituals that were used long ago to decide who was going to be sacrificed to the gods.

It is thought that others may come from rhymes and formulas that wizards used during the Middle Ages to perform acts of magic.

The famous rhyme "Eena, meena, mina, mo," or "Eeny, meeny, miney, mo," is based on an ancient way of counting in the Celtic language that first was used in England perhaps two thousand years ago. "Ina, mina, tethera, methera," the numbers went, or "One, two, three, four." It is said that some English shepherds still use these numbers to count their flocks. And we still use them in our games.

Hide and Seek

Not last night, but the night before,
Forty-four robbers came knocking at my door,
I opened the door and let them in,
Hit them on the head with a rolling pin.
All hid? All hid?

Apples, peaches, pumpkin pie,
Whoever isn't ready
Holler I.

Bushel of wheat,
Bushel of clover,
All ain't ready
Can't hide over.

1, 2, 3,
Look out for me,
I'm going to find you
Wherever you be.

97

Jumping Rope

Miss Lucy had a baby,
She named him Tiny Tim,
She put him in the bathtub
To see if he could swim.

He drank up all the water,
He ate a bar of soap,
He tried to eat the bathtub,
But it wouldn't go down his throat.

Miss Lucy called the doctor,
Miss Lucy called the nurse,
Miss Lucy called the lady
With the alligator purse.

"Mumps," said the doctor,
"Measles," said the nurse,
"Chicken pox," said the lady
With the alligator purse.

Cinderella dressed in yella
Went downtown to meet her fella.
On the way her girdle busted,
How many people were disgusted?
10, 20, 30 . . .

I went downtown
To see Mrs. Brown,
She gave me a nickel
To buy a pickle.
The pickle was sour,
She gave me a flower.
The flower was dead,
She gave me a thread.
The thread was thin,
She gave me a pin.
The pin was sharp,
She gave me a harp.
And the harp began to sing,
"Minnie and a Minnie
And a ha, ha, ha!"

99

Two little sausages
Frying in a pan,
One went POP!
The other went BAM!

Policeman, policeman, do your duty,
Here comes _____, the American beauty,
She can wiggle, she can waggle,
She can do the splits,
She can wear her skirt up to her hips.

Engine, Engine Number Nine
Going down the Chicago line,
Ain't she pretty, don't she shine,
Engine, Engine Number Nine.

Teddy Bear, Teddy Bear went to a party,
Teddy Bear, Teddy Bear thought he was a smarty.
Teddy Bear, Teddy Bear wanted on the phone,
Teddy Bear, Teddy Bear, time to come home.
Teddy Bear, Teddy Bear, go upstairs,
Teddy Bear, Teddy Bear, say your prayers.
Teddy Bear, Teddy Bear, turn out the light,
Teddy Bear, Teddy Bear, say good night.
"Good night."

Charlie Chaplin sat on a pin,
How many inches did it go in?
1, 2, 3 . . .

Stella, Stella, dressed in black,
Sat down on a carpet tack,
Jumped right up and hollered, "Hell!"
How many times did Stella yell?
1, 2, 3 . . .

Little Miss Pinky all dressed in blue
Died last night at a quarter of two.
Before she died, she told me this,
"Darn that rope that made me miss."

*Not too long ago very few girls jumped rope. It was a boys'
game and had just a small number of rhymes. For how it
came to be a girls' game with hundreds of rhymes, see
page 158.*

Clapping

Clap your hands, slap your knees, or clap with a partner.

I ain't been to Frisco,
I ain't been to school,
I ain't been to college,
But I ain't no fool.

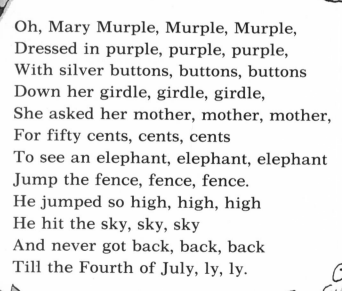

Oh, Mary Murple, Murple, Murple,
Dressed in purple, purple, purple,
With silver buttons, buttons, buttons
Down her girdle, girdle, girdle,
She asked her mother, mother, mother,
For fifty cents, cents, cents
To see an elephant, elephant, elephant
Jump the fence, fence, fence.
He jumped so high, high, high
He hit the sky, sky, sky
And never got back, back, back
Till the Fourth of July, ly, ly.

Pease porridge hot,
Pease porridge cold,
Pease porridge in the pot,
Nine days old.

My brother likes it hot,
My sister likes it cold,
My cat likes it in the pot
Nine days old.

I'm a pretty little Dutch girl
As funny as can be,
And all the boys on my block
Are crazy over me.
My boyfriend's name is Patty,
He comes from Cincinnati
With a pickle on his nose
And corns on his toes.
You ought to hear him laugh
With his ho, ho, ho's,
And that's the way my story goes.

Bouncing a Ball

With some of these rhymes you just bounce a ball. With others you also hop, clap, or touch your toes, or lift your leg over the ball. If two are playing, the first to miss loses.

1, 2, 3, alary,
My first name is Mary,
If it's necessary,
Look it up
In the dictionary.

Red, white and green,
My father is a machine,
My mother is the steering wheel,
And I'm the gasoline.

Sasparilla,
Soda water,
Ginger ale,
Pop,
Lemonade,
Root beer,
Hop, hop, hop.

Bouncie, bouncie ballie,
I broke my new dollie,
My mother came out
And gave me a clout
That turned my petticoat
Inside out.

Oliver Twist can't do this,
So what's the use of trying?
Touch your knee, touch your toe,
Clap your hands,
And around you go.

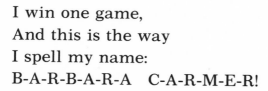

I win one game,
And this is the way
I spell my name:
B-A-R-B-A-R-A   C-A-R-M-E-R!

Fiddling Around

If you repeat this rhyme fast enough and long enough, and keep your voice high enough, you will sound like a fiddle playing.

Ah who dydle de,
Ah who dydle de de,
Ah who dydle de de de,
Ah who dydle de de de—hee hee!

Taking One Breath

Try these rhymes with your friends. The one who continues the longest without taking another breath is the winner.

My father left me, as he was able,
One bowl, one bottle, and one table,
Two bowls, two bottles, and two tables,
Three bowls, three bottles, and three tables . . .

Ninety-nine bottles of beer on the wall,
But what if one of those bottles should fall?
Ninety-eight bottles of beer on the wall,
But what if one of those bottles should fall?
Ninety-seven bottles of beer on the wall . . .

Chanting

Mrs. Sue, Mrs. Sue,
Mrs. Sue from Alabam',
Hey, you! Hey, you!
Sittin' in my rocker
Eatin' Betty Crocker
Watchin' the time go by.
Tick, tock, tick, tock.
A-B-C-D-E-F-G,
Wash those crumbs right off of me,
Moonshine, moonshine—
FREEZE!

Now point to somebody else, who starts again.

This is a dishwashing chant:

Gilly, gilly, gilly, gilly,
WASH! WASH! WASH! WASH!
Kum-ba, kum-ba,
Ya-wa.
Gilly, gilly, gilly, gilly,
WASH! WASH! WASH! WASH!
Kum-ba, kum-ba,
Ya-wa.

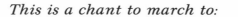

This is a chant to march to:

Left, left,
I had a good wife and I left,
I left my wife and four fat babies
Without any gingerbread.
Hay-foot, straw-foot, belly full of beans.
Left, left . . .

And this is a chant to dance to and clap to:

Ladies and gentlemen,
Children, too,
Us two chicks gonna boogy for you,
Gonna turn around,
Touch the ground,
And shimmy, shimmy, shimmy
All around.
I don't like college,
I don't like school,
But when it comes to boogyin',
I'm an alligatin' fool . . .

Cheering

Strawberry shortcake,
Huckleberry pie,
V-I-C-T-O-R-Y!

Choo, choo! Bang, bang!
Got to get my boomerang.
Ungahwah—got the mighty power!
How we gonna do 'em?
Put your mind to 'em.
Hit 'em in the chest,
Hit 'em like the rest,
Ungahwah—got the mighty power!

A veevo, a vivo,
A veevo, vivo, voom!
Go get a rat trap
Bigger than a bat trap,
Bigger than a cat trap,
BOOM!

❧ 12. Rain and Shine ❧

What will the weather bring?
The rhymes in this chapter will tell you.

A ring around the moon,
Rain is coming soon.

Showery,
Flowery.

Rain, rain, go to Spain,
Never show your face again.

The wind, the wind,
The wind blew high,
The rain comes falling from the sky. . . .

It's raining, it's pouring,
The old man is snoring,
He got into bed and bumped his head
And didn't get up until morning.

What did the blackbird say to the crow?
"It ain't gonna rain no more."
How the heck can I wash my neck
If it ain't gonna rain no more?

Daffy-down-dilly has just come to town
With a yellow petticoat and a green gown.*

*A daffodil.

Blackbird, whistle,
Woodpecker, drum,
Spring has come, spring has come.
Cardinal, sing in the apple tree,
Spring is here for you and me.
Longer day, shorter night,
Little boy, bring out your kite.

Berries red, have no dread,
Berries white, poisonous sight,
Leaves three, quickly flee—
Poison ivy!

Corn knee-high
By the Fourth of July.

Button to the chin,
Autumn's coming in.

Slippy,
Drippy,
Nippy.

The north wind doth blow,
And we shall have snow,
And what will poor robin do then,
poor thing?

Snow, snow faster,
Ally, ally blaster,
The old woman is plucking her geese,
Selling her feathers a penny apiece.

Showery,
Flowery . . .

13. A Tree

And the green grass grew all around,
All around,
And the green grass grew all around. . . .

Tune: *The Green Grass Grew All Around*

In the woods there was a hole, The pret-tiest hole __

__ you e-ver did see, Oh, a hole in the woods, a

hole in the ground, And the green grass grew all a-

-round, All a-round, And the green grass grew all a-round. And

in that hole there was a root, The

pret-tiest root _____ you e-ver did see....

In the woods there was a hole,
The prettiest hole you ever did see,
Oh, a hole in the woods, a hole in the ground,
And the green grass grew all around,
All around,
And the green grass grew all around.

And in that hole there was a root,
Oh, prettiest root you ever did see,
Root in the hole,
Hole in the ground,
And the green grass grew all around,
All around,
And the green grass grew all around.

And on that root there was a tree,
Oh, prettiest tree you ever did see,
Tree on the root,
Root in the hole,
Hole in the ground,
And the green grass grew all around,
All around,
And the green grass grew all around.

And on that tree there was a branch,
Oh, prettiest branch you ever did see,
Branch on the tree,
Tree on the root,
Root in the hole,
Hole in the ground,
And the green grass grew all around,
All around,
And the green grass grew all around.

And on that branch there was a nest,
Oh, prettiest nest you ever did see,
Nest on the branch,
Branch on the tree,
Tree on the root,
Root in the hole,
Hole in the ground,
And the green grass grew all around,
All around,
And the green grass grew all around.

And in that nest there was an egg,
Oh, prettiest egg you ever did see,
Egg in the nest,
Nest on the branch,
Branch on the tree,
Tree on the root,
Root in the hole,
Hole in the ground,
And the green grass grew all around,
All around,
And the green grass grew all around.

And in that egg there was a bird,
Oh, prettiest bird you ever did see,
Bird in the egg,
Egg in the nest,
Nest on the branch,
Branch on the tree,
Tree on the root,
Root in the hole,
Hole in the ground,
And the green grass grew all around,
All around,
And the green grass grew all around.

⚜ 14. Animals and ⚜
Insects

The only things stranger than people are the fish,
dogs, fleas, bees, elephants, and other
creatures in this chapter.

The elephants are coming one by one,
Some from the moon, some from the sun. . . .

Did you ever go fishing on a bright summer day,
Stand on the bank and watch the fishes play,
With your hands in your pockets
And your pockets in your pants,
Watching the fishes
Do a hootchie-kootchie dance?

Tune: *Turkey in the Straw*

Did you ev - er go fish-ing on a bright _ sum-mer day, Stand _

on the bank and watch the fish - es play....

I have a dog,
His name is Rover,
He is a very smart pup.
He stands on his back legs—
If I hold his front legs up.

Tune: *Reuben, Reuben*

I have a dog, His name is Rov-er, He is a ver - y smart _ pup.

I have a dog thin as a rail,
He has fleas all over his tail,
Every time his tail goes flop,
The fleas on the bottom
All hop to the top.

Some people say that fleas are black,
But you know this isn't so,
For Mary had a little lamb
Whose fleas were white as snow.

Mary had a swarm of bees,
And to save their lives,
They went everywhere that Mary went,
For Mary had the hives.

The elephants are coming one by one,
Some from the moon, some from the sun,
Now they are coming two by two,
Some for me, some for you.
Here they come three by three,
Some for you, some for me,
The elephants are coming four by four,
Some through the windows, some through the floor,

Now they are coming five by five,
Some are ghosts, some are alive,
Here they come six by six,
Some on crutches, some on sticks,
The elephants are coming seven by seven,
Some from the moon, some from heaven,
Now they are coming eight by eight,
Some through the windows, some through the gate,
Here they come nine by nine,
Some are yours, some are mine. . . .

On a mule we find two legs behind
And two we find before,
But we must stand behind to find
What the two behind be for.

This little mule, he kicked so high,
I thought that I would reach the sky.

The hyena is a fearsome beast.
Don't go near him, little boys,
Especially when he shakes his tail
And makes this awful noise:

A-ZAH! A-ZAH! A-ZAH!!!

Panthers scream, bobcats squall,
The house cat jumps through a hole in the wall.

The night was dark and stormy,
The billy goat was blind,
He backed into the barbed wire fence,
And scratched his never mind.

Birdie, birdie in the sky,
Why'd you do that in my eye?
I don't whimper, I don't cry,
I'm just glad that cows don't fly.

The firefly is a funny bird,
He hasn't any mind,
He blunders all the way through life
With his headlights on behind.

Oh, say, can you see
Any bedbugs on me?
If you do, pick a few,
And we'll have bedbug stew.

Tune: *The Star-Spangled Banner*

O ___ say, can you see An - y

bed - bugs on me? If you do, pick a

few, And we'll have bed - bug stew. ___

The ants go marching one by one,
Hurrah! Hurrah!
The ants go marching one by one,
Hurrah! Hurrah!
The ants go marching one by one
And the last one stops to have some fun,
And they all go marching
Down and around
And into the ground
To get out of the rain.
Boom, boom, boom, boom,
Boom, boom, boom.

The ants go marching two by two,
Hurrah! Hurrah!
The ants go marching two by two,
Hurrah! Hurrah!
The ants go marching two by two,
And the last one stops to tie his shoe,
And they all go marching
Down and around
And into the ground
To get out of the rain.
Boom, boom, boom, boom,
Boom, boom, boom.

131

The ants go marching three by three,
And the last one stops to climb a tree . . .

The ants go marching four by four,
And the last one stops to close the door . . .

The ants go marching five by five,
And the last one stops to take a dive . . .

The ants go marching six by six,
And the last one stops to pick up sticks . . .

The ants go marching seven by seven,
And the last one stops to go to heaven . . .

The ants go marching eight by eight,
And the last one stops to shut the gate . . .

The ants go marching nine by nine,
And the last one stops and falls behind . . .

The ants go marching ten by ten,
Hurrah! Hurrah!
The ants go marching ten by ten,
Hurrah! Hurrah!
The ants go marching ten by ten,
And the last one stops and shouts, "The End!"
And they all go marching
Down and around
And into the ground
To get out of the rain.
Boom, boom, boom, boom,
Boom, boom, boom.

Tune: *When Johnny Comes Marching Home*

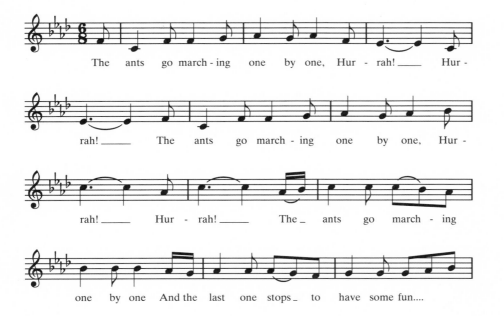

The ants go march-ing one by one, Hur - rah!____ Hur -

rah!____ The ants go march - ing one by one, Hur -

rah!____ Hur - rah!____ The _ ants go march - ing

one by one And the last one stops _ to have some fun....

Be kind to your web-footed friends,
For a duck may be somebody's mother,
She lives all alone in a swamp,
Where it is always cold and damp.
You may think that *this* is the end,
Well, it is.

Tune: *The Stars and Stripes Forever*

⚹ 15. Other Things ⚹

Is there anything else for a folk poet to write about?
Of course. There are prunes, teapots, dentists,
ladybugs, and everything else you can think of.

As wet as a fish, as dry as a bone,
As live as a bird, as dead as a stone,
As hot as an oven, as cold as a frog,
As gay as a lark, as sick as a dog,
As blind as a bat, as deaf as a post,
As cool as a cucumber, as warm as toast . . .

Are you a camel, a big yellow camel?
Do you have a hump?
Do you sit at a table
As straight as you are able?
Or do you sit in a lump, lump, lump?

Let me call you sweetheart,
I'm in love with your machine,
Let me hear you whisper
That you'll buy the gasoline,
Keep your headlights burning
And your hands upon the wheel,
Let me call you sweetheart,
I'm in love with your automobile.

Tune: *Let Me Call You Sweetheart*

Let me call you sweet - heart, I'm in

love with your ma - chine, _____

Let me hear you whis - per That you'll

buy the gas - o - line. _____

Don't steal this book, my little lad,
For five dollars it cost my dad,
And when you die, the Lord will say,
"Where is the book you stole that day?"
And when you say, "I do not know,"
The Lord will say, "Please step below."

We are the boys of Avenue D
You hear so much about,
People hide their pocketbooks
Whenever we go out.
We are noted for our dirty work
In everything we do,
All the coppers hate us,
And so will you.

1, 2, 3, 4, 5, 6, 7
All good children go to heaven,
But those who swear
Don't go there.
1, 2, 3, 4, 5, 6, 7

Old man Moses, sick in bed,
Called the doctor. The doctor said,
"Old man, old man, you ain't sick,
All you need is a licorice stick."

If you have the hiccups, say this as fast as you can:

Hiccup, snickup,
Rise up, kick up,
Three drops in the cup
Are good for the hiccup.

Then take three sips of water from the far side of a cup.

Little seed inside a prune,
Is it night, or is it noon?
What is in there, what you doin'
Little seed inside a prune?

No matter how young a prune may be,
He is always very wrinkled.
A baby prune is like his dad,
Only he's not wrinkled quite so bad.

We all have wrinkles on our face,
But a prune has wrinkles everyplace.
No matter how young a prune may be,
He's always very wrinkled.

Open your mouth and close your eyes,
I'll give you something to make you wise.

Close your eyes and open your hand,
I'll give you something to make you grand.

*When a bucking bronco died in Johnston, Colorado,
cowboys put up a tombstone over his grave with this
poem:*

Under this sod lies a great bucking horse,
There never lived a cowboy he couldn't toss,
His name was Midnight,
He was black as coal,
If there is a hoss heaven,
Please, God, rest his soul.

There is a bend in the Tombigbee River in Alabama where there are wonderful echoes. When a steamboat came around that bend, the deckhands sang "echo songs" they had made up over the years. This was one:

Sound the bell!
Sound the bell!
Let's go down to Carson
To hear the steamboats blow.
The sound falls here,
The sound falls there,
It makes you quiver
Just like the river,
Hear the echo, echo, echo. . . .

The echoes would sound for miles along the riverside.

142

When a big tree falls
And people aren't near,
Does it really make a noise
If no one can hear?

Often we are foolish,
When it's hot we want it coolish,
When it's cool we want it hot,
Always wanting what is not.

Oh, dear, bread and beer,
If I were home, I wouldn't be here.

I'm a little teapot stout,
Here's my handle, here's my spout,
When I get all steamed up, I shout,
"Just tip me over and pour me out!"

Don't worry if your job is small
And if the rewards are few,
Remember that the mighty oak
Was once a nut like you.

A chicken in the car
And the car won't go,
That's the way to spell
Chicago.

A knife and a fork
And a bottle and a cork,
That's the way to spell
New York.

There was an old man from Peru
Who dreamed he was eating his shoe,
He awoke in the night
In a terrible fright,
And found he was eating his shoe.

Daniel was a naughty man,
He would not obey the king.
The king threw him in a dungeon
With lions down beneath,
But Daniel was a dentist
And he pulled the lions' teeth.

My mother is a Russian,
My father is a spy,
I'm a little tattletale
For the FBI.

Little Miss Muffet sat on a tuffet
Eating her curds and whey.
Along came a spider
And sat down beside her,
And asked,
"Is this seat taken?"

Ladybug, ladybug, fly away home.
Your house is on fire,
And your children will burn.
All but one, her name is Ann,
And she crept under the frying pan.

I swapped me a horse and got me a cow,
But when it came to swapping,
I didn't know how.
So I swapped my cow and got me a calf,
But in that trade I got just half.
Then I swapped my calf and got me a pig,
But the poor little thing, it never growed big.
Then I swapped my pig and got me a hen,
But it wouldn't lay an egg even now and then.
Then I swapped my hen and got me a cat,
But the pretty little thing by the chimney sat.

Then I swapped my cat and got me a mouse,
But his tail caught fire, and he burned down the house.
Then I swapped my mouse and got me a mole,
But the dad-burned thing went right down its hole.

Good night,
Sleep tight,
Don't let the bedbugs bite.

Notes

Sources

Bibliography

Index of First Lines

Abbreviations in Notes, Sources and Bibliography

AA	*American Anthropologist*
HF	*Hoosier Folklore*
IUA	Indiana University Folklore Archive, Bloomington, Ind.
JAF	*Journal of American Folklore*
KFQ	*Keystone Folklore Quarterly*
MAFS	*Memoirs of the American Folklore Society*
MF	*Midwest Folklore*
NCFJ	*North Carolina Folklore Journal*
NEFA	Northeast Folklore Archive, Orono, Me.
NWF	*Northwest Folklore*
NYFA	Folklore Archive, New York State Historical Association, Cooperstown, N.Y.
NYFQ	*New York Folklore Quarterly*
PTFS	Publications of Texas Folklore Society
RU	Compiler's collection of folklore, contributed by his students at Rutgers University, New Brunswick, N.J., 1963–78.
SFQ	*Southern Folklore Quarterly*
TSLL	*Texas Studies in Language and Literature*
UM	University of Massachusetts folklore collection, Amherst, Mass.
UMA	University of Maryland Folklore Archive, College Park, Md.
UPA	University of Pennsylvania Folklore Archive, Philadelphia, Pa.
UTA	University of Texas archive of student folklore collections, Barker Center for Texas History, Austin, Tex.

WF	*Western Folklore*
WPA	WPA Folklore Archive, Library of Congress, assembled during the economic depression of the 1930s. Collectors were unemployed folklorists and writers hired by the United States government.
WSUA	Wayne State University Folklore Archive, Detroit, Mich.

Notes

The publications mentioned are described in the Bibliography.

Folk Poets and Folk Poetry. A folk poet made up each of the poems in this book. As the poem moved by word of mouth from place to place, other folk poets changed it. Often they wanted to improve it or had something they wanted to add. In some cases they kept just the form of the poem or a tune to which it was sung and created a completely new version. The jump-rope rhyme "Cinderella" is a good example of this. There are now a dozen rhymes about her life and love affairs, including the rhyme in Chapter 11. In the beginning there was just one.

Although most folk poets are unknown, there are a few whose names we do know. Usually these are local poets who write about real or imaginary events where they live and whose poems become part of the folklore in their town or neighborhood. Orin Pullen of Amity, Maine, was one such poet. His poem about a pig gone wild is retold in Amity and also in Chapter 8.

Sometimes a folk poet records the events in his family, and these poems become part of the family lore that is passed down. In one family in Clearfield County, Pennsylvania, there were family poets for almost a hundred years. They wrote about a Model-T Ford, a wild night on a steam locomotive, their school days, jobs and hard times, and other family matters that have become legend.

There are great differences between folk poetry and literary poetry. A literary poem is intended to be read silently, to be shared with a reader in the privacy of a printed page. A folk poem is intended to be spoken or sung or performed in some other way. It needs a performer as well as a poet to give it its special quality. This is as true of a jump-rope rhyme as it is of a camp song.

There is another difference. Literary poets try to use beautiful language to express their ideas about life. Folk poets use the everyday language ordinary people use. See Paredes; Baldwin.

153

Street Rhymes (Introduction). These are one of the major kinds of children's folklore, and they have many uses. The sounds and silliness these rhymes contain are, of course, a source of fun. But they also regulate games through choosing who will be It, announcing the rules to be observed, and providing a rhythm for ball bouncing, hand clapping, and rope jumping. Through taunts and other rhymes, they also set rules for how others should behave. In addition, they help children express their feelings more easily.

The scholar Robbins Burling has found that children use the same kinds of street rhymes no matter where they live or what language they speak. The ideas are the same, and so are the four-line stanzas they use with four stressed beats to each line. This was the case, he learned, with children who speak such unrelated languages as English; Arabic; Yoruba, in Nigeria; Trukese, in the south Pacific; and Serrano, an Indian language spoken in southern California. See Farb, pp. 134–36.

Nursery Rhymes (Introduction). These are the rhymes that parents teach their young children. When these children are grown, often they teach them to their children. They include "Little Jack Horner," "Jack Sprat," "Jack and Jill" and hundreds of other traditional rhymes. But children seldom learn these from one another, for they were created by adults and they do not meet a child's needs when he or she goes out into his world.

Many of these nursery rhymes are English and date from the nineteenth century. But some go back to the seventeenth and eighteenth centuries and earlier. A number are early songs from games that adults played. Others are from ballads, folk songs, popular songs of the day, political songs, and stage plays.

As a result, a surprising number of nursery rhymes are concerned with violence, cruelty, and immoral behavior. Since children in the past were regarded as miniature adults, no one saw anything wrong with this. But these rhymes also include charms, riddles, nonsense verse, lullabies, and exercises to help children learn letters and numbers; often these are delightful. Opie, *Dictionary,* pp. 1–11; Bar-ing–Gould, 11–21.

Parodies (Chapters 1–6, 14, 15). Children everywhere use parodies, just as the ancient Greeks did. Like writers of old, they use them to make fun of ideas they don't agree with and writing that strikes them as silly.

One of their targets is nursery rhymes, such as the parodies of "Mary Had a Little Lamb" in Chapter 2 and "Little Miss Muffet" in Chapter 15. They are one means children use to point out that they no longer are at their mother's knee.

Advertising commercials are another popular subject for attack. Here are two examples:

> Pepsi-Cola hits the spot,
> Ties your belly in a knot!

> Sani-Flush, Sani-Flush,
> Cleans your teeth without a brush!

And there are hundreds more. They reflect findings of studies show-ing that children are cynical about advertising claims. It is not the products that bother them. It is the commercials.

The parodies of folk songs, carols, and hymns on which the anti-school songs in Chapter 3 are based are a different matter. In this case, children are not making fun of the songs, but are using them to express their feelings about another subject. "On Top of Old Smoky" is one song they use in this way. But there also is a real parody of the song in Chapter 2—"On Top of Spaghetti"—which makes fun of the sentimental lyrics in the original.

With this and other poems, we often learn the parody before we learn the original. See Esar, pp. 233–36; Knapp, pp. 161–79; Krueger; Loomis, "Mary"; Monteiro.

Autograph Rhymes (Chapters 1, 4, 6). The custom of keeping an autograph album in which friends wrote comments seems to have begun with university students in Germany in the sixteenth and seventeenth centuries. The album was called a "book of friends." Over the years it became a *Stammbuch*, a family album in which friends, relatives, and family members all wrote their thoughts on important occasions.

By the 1850s German immigrants had brought the custom to America and England. Those who wrote in these albums in those years used quotations from some poets or philosophers or the Bible and signed their names. When people stopped using quotations and started making up their own comments, all sorts of folk rhymes began to appear. At first they were rather serious, but as writing in autograph albums became more of a children's custom the rhymes became more lively:

> I wish I were a cabbage,
> I'd cut myself in two.
> To all my friends I'd give a leaf,
> But I'd give my heart to you.
>
> May our friendship spread
> Like hot butter on gingerbread.
>
> It tickles me,
> It makes me laugh
> To think you want
> My autograph.

Emrich, "Autograph"; Randolph, "Autograph Albums," pp. 182–83; Brewster.

Nonsense (Chapter 9). One of the common ways to create nonsense is by reversing ordinary ideas and roles. This famous rhyme is an example:

> One bright day in the middle of the night,
> Two dead men got up to fight.

We also can create nonsense by reversing words ("Twas in the month of Liverpool,/ In the city of July . . .") or letters ("Once a big mollicepan/Saw a bittle lum") or by repeating something endlessly ("Who threw the overalls in Mrs. Murphy's chowder?"). And there are many other methods.

In a world of nonsense, everything becomes something that makes no sense in the usual way. As this happens we move further and further from the guidelines we use in our normal lives. Doing so helps us decide what common sense really is. See Stewart; Opie, *Lore*, p. 24; Schwartz, *Tomfoolery*, p. 67, *Flapdoodle*, p. 29.

Poetry About Work (Chapters 7, 15). "When I Came to This Land," in Chapter 7, is a poem about the struggles of work. Workers also have created songs to protest poor working conditions. And their children have created jump-rope and ball-bouncing rhymes about labor unions and strikes, like these from the 1930s:

> Wages up and hours down,
> Make Chicago a union town.

> Father's on the picket line,
> Mother will walk in clover,
> Baby will get milk so fine
> When the strike is over.

Some poetry about work consists of just a few words that workers chanted or sang as they labored. As they cut a crop or tried to lift a load, they repeated the words again and again. In Georgia it was as simple as these examples:

> Everybody bow down,
> Put your hands to it!

> Get it up!
> Get it up!
> Any way to get it up!

With a strong, steady rhythm, the words became a folk poem that helped to get the work done.

The farmers who came to Minnesota from Finland used an ancient chant in their work. As they always had done, they grazed their cows in wild pastures. To be sure they returned, they fed salt from a cowbell to the cow that led the herd. Then they fastened the bell to the cow's neck and chanted in Finnish:

> . . . You are the strongest of my cattle,
> The strongest of my calves,
> Bring ye home the herd
> Clanking to the farmyard. . . .
>
> WPA Folklore Archive

Counting-Out Rhymes (Chapter 11). Most players allow these rhymes to decide who is going to be It. But some arrange things so that *they* decide, not the rhymes. There are many strategies they may follow.

When they reach the end of a rhyme, they may continue reciting, adding "Out goes you!" or "My mother told me to choose this one!" or other endings until they reach the person they want or avoid the person they don't want.

Or they use a rhyme with just the number of beats they need for their strategy. Or they recite a rhyme so that it has more or fewer beats. Or they skip themselves in counting, if that is helpful. Or they choose the last person who is counted out instead of the first. See Goldstein, pp. 170–78.

Jumping Rope (Chapter 11). If a boy jumps rope these days, usually it is only to train for an athletic event. But until the late nineteenth century jumping rope was mostly a boys' activity. They concentrated on solo jumping—on tricks and speed and how high they could jump. Some girls also jumped rope, but like the boys they jumped alone.

There were few jump-rope rhymes in those years. During the

1880s only one was reported by the great collector of children's folklore William Newell. It was this:

> The Bible is a holy and visible law,
> I marry this Indian to this squaw,
> By the point of my jack-knife
> I pronounce you man and wife.

Instead of jumping rope, most girls played singing games such as Little Sally Waters and Miss Jenny Jones, in which they marched, sang, and chanted as they reenacted a story. But as growing numbers of people moved from farms to cities, these games were replaced by jumping rope and ball bouncing.

There were several reasons for this. The paved streets and playgrounds in the cities made it easier to play such games. So did the shorter skirts girls had begun wearing. At that time girls also were being encouraged to exercise more and learn physical skills. When jumping rope, most turned to group jumping, in which two players turned a rope while one or more jumped. As these changes took place, the play rhymes we use today began to appear.

But as more girls became involved, fewer boys did. By the 1920s jumping rope was almost completely a girls' game. See Abrahams, *Jump-Rope*, xv–xviii; Newell, p. 252; Sutton-Smith, pp. 73–74; Turner, pp. 133–35.

Poetry About Current Events (Chapter 15). When a war breaks out or there is an important election or some other important event, one soon may hear folk poetry about what average people think. The rhyme that begins "My mother is a Russian . . ." (p. 145) is one of these poems. This jump-rope rhyme about the long war in Vietnam is another:

> My father went to war, war, war
> In nineteen hundred and sixty-four, four, four,
> He brought me back a gun, gun, gun
> And the gun went—*BANG!*

During an election for President of the United States one may hear these rhymes:

> You'll wonder where your money went
> If _____ is President.

> _____ is in the White House,
> Just been elected.

> _____ is in the garbage can
> Waiting to be collected.

There is also this folk poem about beaches and other lands that the public no longer can use because they are now privately owned. It is a parody of the song "This Land Is Your Land."

> This land is my land,
> This land's not your land.
> I've got a shotgun—
> And you don't have one;
> If you don't get off,
> I'll blast your head off,
> This land was made for only me.

"My father," various sources, 1980s; "You'll wonder," New Brunswick, N.J., RU, 1969; "White House," various sources, late nineteenth, twentieth centuries; "This land," Detroit suburbs, WSUA, 1980.

Sources

The sources of each item are given with variants and related information. The names of informants (I) and collectors (C) are given when available. Publications cited are described in the Bibliography.

1. PEOPLE

p. 1   *Fudge, fudge.* See citation below.

p. 2   *First a daughter; First a son.* Traditional rhymes.

p. 2   *Fudge, fudge.* Quincy, Ill., 1938, WPA. Widespread variant:

> Fudge, fudge, call the judge,
> Mother's got a newborn baby.
> It can't be a boy, it can't be a girl,
> It's just an ordinary baby.
> Wrap it up in tissue paper,
> Send it down the elevator. . . .

p. 2   *I was my mother's.* I: Lavonne Riener, Seward, Neb., 1970s.

p. 3   *Oh, policeman, policeman.* New York City, 1938, WPA.

p. 3   *Down by the ocean.* Widely known. Variant: "Johnny (or Charlie) over the water/ Johnny over the sea . . ." Charlie was Bonnie Prince Charles Stuart, who tried and failed to claim the English throne in the eighteenth century, then spent his life "over the sea," roaming about Europe.

p. 3   *My father is a butcher.* New York City, 1939, WPA. Variants: hot dog, wiener.

p. 4   *My mother, your mother.* New York City counting-out rhyme, WPA, 1938. Widespread variant:

> My mother and your mother
> Were hanging out the clothes
> My mother socked your mother

Right in the nose.
"What color was the blood?"
Red.
R-E-D spells red—and you are *out!*

p. 4   *Katalena.* Excerpt from a hand-clapping rhyme which also describes how Katalena looked:

> She had two eyes in her head,
> One was green, the other was red. . . .
> She had twelve hairs upon her head,
> Six were alive, six were dead. . . .

I: Marcia Gaerte, age 14, Macy, Ind., 1969, IUA.

p. 5   *My name is Yon Yonson.* Traditional endless story.

p. 5   *On the mountain.* I: A. Lucas, Austin, Tex., 1962, UTA.

p. 6   *Do your ears hang low?* I: Jerrilyn Lassiter, age 11, Windfall, Ind., 1968, IUA.

p. 7   *When God gave out noses.* I: Barbara Stover, Grosse Pointe, Mich., n.d., IUA.

p. 8   *I would reduce.* Editor's recollection.

p. 8   *Jerry Hall.* Belmont School, Philadelphia, 1971. In older versions a rat could eat him.

p. 8   *Little dabs of powder.* New York City, 1939, WPA.

p. 9   *After the ball.* Parody of a song popular before World War I. UMA, 1970. For an English version, see Opie, *Lore*, p. 91.

p. 10   *I with I wath a fith.* Editor's recollection, Ten Mile River Boy Scout Camp, Narrowsburg, N.Y., 1940. Fowke has a Canadian version in *Sally,* No. 380.

p. 11   *Violetta in the pantry.* A Maryland version of a poem in a 1796 English story, "The Mimic" by Maria Edgeworth. The first line was "Violante in the pantry." In other versions "Hannah Bantry" and a cat have become the culprits. Whitney, No. 2616; Baring-Gould, No. 321. Adapted slightly.

p. 12   *Gene, Gene.* Widespread nineteenth-century taunting rhyme.

p. 12   *Anna Elise.* A nursery rhyme from perhaps the early twentieth century, similar to an earlier rhyme: "There was a man, he went mad,/ He jumped into a paper bag...." Opie, *Dictionary,* p. 55. An American version used as a jump-rope rhyme begins:

> Anthy Maria (or Obadiah) jumped in the fire.
> The fire was hot, she jumped in the pot . . .

p. 13   *There was a fellow.* Widely known jump-rope rhyme. Variant:

> Three little children all dressed in white,
> Tried to get to heaven on the end of a kite.
> The kite string broke, down they fell,
> Instead of heaven, they went to ——
> Now don't get excited . . .

p. 14   *There was a girl.* I: Avik Roy, age 13, Detroit Country Day School, Detroit area, 1986.

p. 14   *Tell me quick.* Autograph rhyme. I: Shannon English, Kokomo, Ind., 1968, IUA.

p. 14   *The grapes hang green.* Emrich, "Autograph," p. 4.

2. FOOD

p. 15   *Here I stand.* I: Martha Wall, Wallburg, N.C., 1941, Brewster, "Children's," p. 193.

p. 16   *Ravioli.* I: Sara Wood, Kokomo, Ind., 1968, IUA.

p. 18   *On top of spaghetti.* I: Shirley DeWolfe, Sandy Vollback, Amy Johnson, Royal Oak, Mich., 1969, WSUA.

p. 20   *Tomatoes, lettuce.* Green Street School, Philipsburg, N.J., 1978. Offspring of a soup commercial.

p. 20   *I eat my peas.* I: Carietta M. Arvis, Hudson, Mich., 1949, IUA.

p. 20   *Mary had a little lamb.* A combination of two versions: the first four lines, Merry Wilson, Kokomo, Ind., 1969; the remainder, Carietta M. Arvis, Hudson, Mich., 1949; both IUA.

p. 21   *Mary ate some marmalade.* Widespread use in England.

p. 22   *When I found a mouse.* Editor's recollection.

p. 22   *Oh, my.* I: Lynette Beachy, Scottsdale, Pa., 1979, IUA.

p. 23   *Some gum, chum?* Mabel Baron School, Stockton, Cal., 1979.

p. 23   *I scream.* Widely known.

p. 23   *Through the teeth.* Various archives.

p. 23   *Better to urp.* UMA, 1970.

p. 24   *Now I lay me down.* A popular parody of a widespread bedtime verse:

> Now I lay me down to sleep,
> I pray the Lord my soul to keep.
> And if I die before I wake,
> I pray the Lord my soul to take.

The verse may first have appeared in print in 1737 in *The New-England Primer.* Monteiro cites several Rhode Island parodies, p. 44, among them:

> Now I lay me down to sleep,
> My hotrod parked across the street.
> If it should roll before I wake,
> I pray the Lord to use the brake.

p. 24   *Just plant a watermelon.* I: Naomi Feldman, Houston, Tex., 1960s, UTA.

3. SCHOOL

p. 25   *Row, row, row your boat.* Widespread school rhyme.

p. 26   *Heigh-ho.* I: Jennifer Pool, age 9, Colonial Heights School, Stockton, Cal., 1979. See variant cited below, p. 29.

p. 26   *Running to school.* Partial version of New York City jump-rope rhyme, 1939, WPA, concluding: "... First grade/ Second grade/ Third grade .../ C-O-L-L-E-G-E!"

p. 26   *Here comes teacher with a ... stick.* C: Jane C. Twombly, Amherst, Mass., 1972, UM.

4. TEASES AND TAUNTS

> Crybaby, crybaby,
> Sit-and-wonder-why-baby.

p. 34 *Cowardy, cowardy custard.* Primarily a Canadian and English taunt. Waugh, p. 61; Opie, *Lore*, pp. 185–86.

p. 34 *Liar, liar.* I: James Koch, Hamilton, Ohio, 1981.

p. 34 *Cross my heart.* Paterson, N.J., 1973, RU. Variant ending: "Cut my throat if I tell a lie."

p. 34 *Shame, shame.* I: Timmy Baranoff, Austin, Tex., n.d., UTA.

p. 35 *There is a girl.* Primarily a Canadian and English taunt. See Fowke, *Sally,* p. 231; Opie, *Lore*, p. 175.

p. 35 *Tattletale.* Widespread use. A two-hundred-year-old variant:

> Tell-tale tit,
> Your tongue shall be slit,
> And all the dogs in town
> Shall have a bit of it.

p. 35 *Stare, stare.* Editor's childhood recollection, Brooklyn, N.Y., 1930s.

p. 35 *Fat, fat.* Paterson, N.J., 1973, RU.

p. 35 *Skinny bone.* Editor's childhood recollection, Brooklyn, N.Y., 1930s.

p. 36 *Roses are red, Cabbages.* I: Eileen LeDrew, Amherst, Mass., 1972, UM.

p. 36 *Roses are red . . . Do me.* I: Janice Baker, age 10, Greece, N.Y., 1965, in Winslow, "Annotated," p. 169.

p. 36 *Roses are red . . . A face.* I: Eileen LeDrew, Amherst, Mass., 1972, UM.

p. 37 *I love you.* I: Mary Wood, age 14, Kokomo, Ind., 1968, IUA.

p. 37 *Mind your own business.* Rutherford, N.J., 1973, RU.

p. 37 *Too bad, so sad.* I: Rosemary Newman, San Antonio, Tex., 1963, UTA.

p. 37 *I'm the boss.* Rutherford, N.J., 1973, RU.

p. 37 *No way, José.* Denver, Colo., 1987.

p. 37 *Jane, Jane.* New York City, 1938, WPA.

p. 38 *Willie, Willie.* Poplar Bluff, Mo., 1940s, in Musick, p. 435.

p. 38 *Robert, Bedobert.* Northfield, Mass., 1938, WPA.

p. 38 *Susie, Susie Sauerkraut.* Editor's childhood recollection, Brooklyn, N.Y., 1930s. Also a New York City rhyme at the turn of the century, Stimson, p. 125.

p. 38 *There she goes.* New York City, WPA, 1930s; also in Stimson, p. 127.

p. 39 *Twinkle, twinkle.* Mabel Baron School, Stockton, Cal., 1979.

p. 39 *Silence in the court.* C: Gail P. Williams, Philadelphia, 1964, UPA.

p. 40 *You call me names?* Mabel Baron School, Stockton, Cal., 1979.

p. 40 *See my pinky?* I: Robert O. Warren, New York City, 1988.

p. 40 *Sticks and stones.* New York City, 1938, WPA.

p. 40 *Understand, rubber band?* UMA, 1968.

5. WISHES—AND WARNINGS

p. 41 *Needles, pins.* See citation below.

p. 42 *If your shoelace.* Traditional rhyme.

p. 42 *Step on a spoon.* Ohio belief, Hand, *Compendium*, No. 13097.

p. 42 *Step on a knife.* As above.

p. 42 *If your nose itches.* Randolph, *Ozark Magic*, p. 51.

p. 43 *If you sneeze.* Traditional rhyme.

p. 43 *See a pin.* Widely known. New England variant, Johnson, p. 58:

> See a pin and let it lie,
> You'll want that pin before you die.

p. 44 *Count the birds.* I: Ruby Hilliker, Toronto, 1961, WSUA. Magpie used in original text. Compiler has substituted "birds" from other versions.

p. 45 *Fortune-teller.* Widespread use, with varying occupations. Some versions start, "Gypsy, gypsy."

p. 45 *Needles, pins.* I: J. M. Harpham, Albany, N.Y., 1940s, NYFA. Schwartz, *Cross Your Fingers*, has a similar version, p. 48.

p. 46   *I wish.* Rutherford, N.J., 1973, RU; a similar Georgia rhyme in Ford, p. 111.

p. 46   *Touch blue.* Widespread belief. At Franklin School, Detroit, the reverse was reported:

> Touch blue,
> Never come true,

1946, WSUA.

6. Love and Marriage

p. 47   *Somebody loves you.* UMA, 1970.

p. 48   *He is handsome.* New York City jump-rope rhyme, 1938, WPA. MacThomáis reports an Irish version with "Dublin City" in the rhyme. Heck, p. 19, reports this variant:

> She is handsome, she is pretty,
> She is the belle of New York City,
> She has a lover, one, two, three!
> Please come and tell me who she may be.

p. 48   *Down by the river.* Widespread use. Babcock reports this Washington, D.C., variant from the 1880s:

> Down by the river where the green grass grows,
> There sat _____ as pretty as a rose,
> She sang, she sang, she sang herself to sleep,
> And up came _____
> And kissed her on the cheek.

p. 48   *Beneath a shady tree.* I: Miledge H. Lewis, Lubec, Me., 1963, NEFA.

p. 49   *Some kiss behind a lily.* Emrich, "Autograph," p. 6.

p. 49   *I never saw such eyes.* I: Thelma Muncie, St. Cloud, Minn., about 1960, IUA.

p. 49   *Two on a hammock.* Widespread autograph rhyme.

p. 50   *Sister has a boyfriend.* Britt, p. 299. Based on "I Wonder Why," a popular song of the 1920s. Adapted slightly.

p. 50   *I wish I had a nickel.* New York City ball-bouncing rhyme, 1938, WPA.

p. 51   *I wish my mother.* The last lines of an Irish jump-rope rhyme from Belfast. Butler, p. 90.

p. 51   *I love that black-eyed boy.* I: Etta Kilgore, Wise, Va., 1940s, UPA. There are many verses:

> His eyes are blue and he is so true.
> His eyes are brown and he lives in town.
> His eyes are gray and he is so gay.

p. 51   *My heart is not a plaything.* Emrich, "Autograph," p. 6, adapted slightly.

p. 51   *Read up and down.* I: Frankie Ferrar, Chicago, 1953, IUA.

p. 52   *Love many, trust few.* Various archives.

p. 52   *As sure as a vine grows round a stump.* Various sources.

p. 52   *As sure as a vine grows round a rafter.* Floyd County, Ky., 1938, WPA.

p. 53   *I love you.* Chase, p. 219.

p. 53   *Roses red.* Talley, p. 128.

p. 54   *Nobody loves me.* Widespread use with many variants.

p. 54   *Anna and Frankie.* Tompkins Square Park, New York City, 1930s, WPA.

p. 55   *Here comes the bride.* I: Shelda Hoffman, age 10, San Antonio, Tex., 1968, UTA.

p. 56   *Sam and Joan.* I: John H. Schwartz, age 10, Princeton, N.J., 1965.

p. 56   *I wish you luck.* Howard, *Folk Jingles,* Chapter 10, No. 21.

7. WORK

p. 57   *When I first came.* Variant of a Pennsylvania German cumulative song. I: Nancy Conant, Orono, Me., 1962; learned at a University of Maine fraternity party, NEFA. See version in Brendle and Troxell, pp. 68–71; Dorson, pp. 157–58.

8. STORIES

9. NONSENSE

Ephrata, Pa., 1980; Sandra Stolz, Austin, Tex., 1961, UTA, who learned hers in three Texas children's camps; and the editor's recollections.

p. 76   *Oh, the cow kicked.* Widespread circular jingle.

p. 77   *A barefoot boy.* One of several variants of a traditional crazy song. I: Mrs. H. H. Mullenix, Farmington, Ark., 1941, in Randolph, *Ozark Folk Songs,* p. 204. Abridged. For two other versions, see Schwartz, *Tomfoolery,* p. 66.

p. 78   *Who put the overalls.* Widespread circular jingle.

p. 79   *Mama, Mama.* Nonsense version of a traditional lullaby. W. 27th St. and 9th Ave., New York City, 1939, WPA.

p. 80   *I'm up here.* Traditional "tangletalk" song, I: Carol Waldman, Philadelphia, recollection from Camp Echo, Burlington, N.Y., 1956–58, UPA. Variant: Schwartz, *Tomfoolery*, p. 63.

p. 82   *Boom, boom.* Widespread crazy song.

p. 84   *As I was going out.* UMA, 1970.

10. RIDDLES

p. 85   *Four stiff-standers.* Found throughout the world with many variants.

p. 86   *What is the difference.* Albany, N.Y., 1940s, NYFA.

p. 86   *As I was going to St. Ives.* Once a favorite in Laurium in northernmost Michigan, where many came from the fishing village of St. Ives in Cornwall, England, that is mentioned in the rhyme. Laurium, Mich., 1937, WPA.

p. 87   *Round and round.* Traditional riddle–tongue twister.

p. 87   *What is it you always see. Puzzledom*, p. 112, No. 98.

p. 87   *Light as a feather.* Missouri, 1930s, WPA.

p. 88   *Thirty white cows.* Widely known with many versions. A seventeenth-century variant, Opie, *Dictionary*, p. 212:

> Four and twenty white bulls
> Sate upon a stall,

Forth came the red bull
And licked them all.

p. 88   *Feed it.* I: Edwin Knowlton, Stonington, Me., 1975.

p. 88   *The first letter.* New Brunswick, N.J., 1970. For a Canadian version, see Fowke, *Ring*, p. 30.

p. 89   *Many eyes.* North Carolina, 1930s, WPA.

p. 89   *It stays all year.* C: Muriel M. Siegel, Franklin School, Detroit, 1946, WSUA.

p. 89   *It runs all day.* Widely known.

p. 89   *Flies forever.* UMA, 1970.

p. 89   *A snow-white bird.* Traditional snow riddle.

p. 90   *I saw a peacock.* Halliwell-Phillips, p. 79. A traditional riddle designed to improve punctuation. For others, see Opie, *Family*, pp. 106–107; Schwartz, *Flapdoodle*, pp. 84–85, and *Unriddling*, pp. 40–41.

p. 91   *In the beginning.* Editor's recollection.

p. 91   *And now, sir.* Traditional challenge.

11. Fun and Games

p. 93   *One for the money.* Traditional race-starting rhyme.
A descendant of:

> "One to make ready
> And two to prepare;
> Good luck to the rider,
> And away goes the mare.

Baring-Gould, p. 259.

p. 94   *When I went up the apple tree.* Widespread use, with many variants. See Newell, p. 203, New England; Maryott, p. 56, Nebraska; Yoffie, p. 28, St. Louis.

p. 94   *Intie, mintie, tootsie, lala.* I: Nola Johnson, Yarmouth, Me., 1967, NEFA. A descendant of "Intery, mintery, cutery, corn," in use two centuries ago. See "Counting-Out Rhymes" in Notes.

p. 94 *Monkey, monkey.* Widespread use.

p. 95 *Wire, briar, limberlock.* Traditional rhyme with deep roots. Musick, p. 427, Missouri; Perrow, p. 142, Mississippi. Some variants begin "William A. Trimbletoe/ Catches hens, puts them in pens . . ."

p. 95 *Eeny, meeny, miney, mo.* Perrow, p. 140. Spelling adjusted.

p. 96 *Yellow cornmeal.* I: Ann Wharton, East Texas region, 1930s, in Howard, *Folk Jingles*, Chapter 13, No. 31; also Houston, 1960s, UTA.

p. 97 *Not last night.* Highland Heights Elementary School, Houston, Tex., 1937, WPA.

p. 97 *Apples, peaches.* I: Janice M. Kagarise, Philadelphia, 1964; a rhyme in her family since at least 1912, UPA.

p. 97 *Bushel of wheat.* Widespread in southeastern United States.

p. 97 *1, 2, 3.* Mississippi, 1930s, WPA. Variant ending: "You'd better hide before I can see," Perrow, p. 141.

p. 98 *Miss Lucy had a baby.* I: Cheryl Marks, Detroit, 1974, WSUA.

p. 99 *Cinderella.* Widely known, with many variants: She goes upstairs to kiss her fella, goes downstairs to bake some bread, goes downtown to buy an umbrella, dresses in lace, powders her face, has her garters or bloomers "bust."

p. 99 *I went downtown.* Widespread use.

p. 100 *Two little sausages.* UMA, 1970.

p. 100 *Policeman, policeman.* Widespread use. Also ends, "She can dance, she can sing,/ She can do most anything," Abrahams, *Jump-Rope,* p. 161.

p. 100 *Engine, Engine Number Nine.* Gregory Elementary School, Houston, Tex., 1938, WPA.

p. 100 *Teddy Bear, Teddy Bear.* Berkeley, Cal., 1943, Clair, "Berkeley," pp. 278–9, 1954, adapted slightly. Most versions start, "Teddy Bear, Teddy Bear, turn around,/ Teddy Bear, Teddy Bear, touch the ground."

p. 101 *Charlie Chaplin.* Willamantic, Conn., 1930s, WPA.

p. 101 *Stella, Stella.* Arkansas, 1933, in Randolph, "Arkansas," p. 78.

p. 101 *Little Miss Pinky.* I: Mary Ellen McLeod, age 7, Detroit area, 1964, WSUA.

p. 102 *I ain't been to Frisco.* Newark, N.J., 1973, RU.

p. 102 *Oh, Mary Murple.* Detroit, 1976, C: Sharon Chaney, WSUA. Widespread variant:

> Mary Mack, Mack, Mack,
> Dressed in black, black, black,
> Silver buttons all down,
> Her back, back, back.

Based on an old riddle which described a commonly used black coffin decorated with button-like objects. Taylor, p. 234.

p. 103 *Pease porridge hot.* New York City, 1930s, WPA. A variant of the traditional nursery rhyme which concludes "Some like it hot . . ." At one time used with a clapping game children played on cold days to keep their hands warm. Pease porridge was a thin English pudding made from pease meal, or ground peas. See Opie, *Dictionary*, p. 345; Baring-Gould, pp. 239–40.

p. 103 *I'm a pretty little Dutch girl.* UMA, 1970. Variants: Instead of "Fatty from Cincinnati," "Sammy from Alabamy," "Sambo from Alabamo," "Randy from the land of candy."

p. 104 *1, 2, 3, alary.* Widespread use.

p. 104 *Red, white and green.* Editor's recollection.

p. 104 *Sasparilla.* I: Isabel Malloy, Rye, N.Y., 1940s, NYFA. "Sarsaparilla" is the standard spelling.

p. 105 *Bouncie, bouncie ballie.* Widespread use.

p. 105 *Oliver Twist.* I: Carolyn Brumm, Rye, N.Y., 1940s, NYFA.

p. 105 *I win one game.* I: Barbara Carmer Schwartz, childhood recollection, Delmar, N.Y., 1930s.

p. 106 *Ah who dydle de.* I: Henry Walker, Hazen, Ark., 1930s, WPA. Although collected in Arkansas, the chant is known as a "Georgia whoop." Spelling adapted for clarity.

p. 106 *My father left me.* A nineteenth-century nursery rhyme.

p. 107 *Ninety-nine bottles.* A twentieth-century version, now sung in reverse. In a Texas variant, "Take one down and pass it around."

p. 107 *Mrs. Sue.* I: Cala A. Edelstein, age 10, Winchester-Thurston School, Pittsburgh, Pa., 1983.

p. 108 *Gilly, gilly.* I: Elizabeth Robbins, Silsbee, Tex., 1981, UTA.

p. 108 *Left, left.* I: Barbara Carmer Schwartz, childhood recollection, Delmar, N.Y., 1930s. The terms "hay-foot, straw-foot" are said to have been used by New York State soldiers during the American Revolutionary War. According to legend, some tied a wisp of hay to the left foot and a wisp of straw to the right. That way they could tell their left foot from their right in marching drills.

p. 109 *Ladies and gentlemen.* C: Sharon Chaney, Detroit, 1960, WSUA. Abridged.

p. 110 *Strawberry shortcake.* UMA, 1970.

p. 110 *Choo, choo.* Detroit, 1960s, WSUA.

p. 110 *A veevo.* New York City, 1930s, WPA. Stimson reports a similar cheer from New York during the years 1893–1903, p. 128. An Ozark song from the same period ends, ". . . Go get a rat-trap, go get a cat-trap, go get a rat-trap bigger than a cat-trap," Randolph, *Ozark Folk Songs*, p. 154. In the 1940s the editor cheered teams at Erasmus Hall High School, Brooklyn, N.Y., with:

> "Veevo, vivo,
> veevo, vess,
> E-R-A-S-M-U-S!"

12. RAIN AND SHINE

p. 111 *A ring around the moon.* Traditional weather rhyme.

p. 112 *Showery.* See citation below.

p. 112 *Rain, rain.* New Brunswick, N.J., 1970, RU. In his 1659 book

Proverbs, James Howell reported "Raine, raine, goe to Spain: faire weather come againe," Opie, *Lore*, p. 218.

p. 112   *The wind, the wind.* From an Irish jump-rope rhyme, Butler, p. 95. Also see Heck, No. 24.

p. 113   *It's raining.* Widespread use, although possibly not known before 1930s. Opie, *Lore*, p. 219.

p. 113   *What did the blackbird.* A verse to the square-dance tune "It Ain't Gonna Rain No More."

p. 113   *Daffy-down-dilly.* Nineteenth-century riddling rhyme.

p. 114   *Blackbird, whistle.* Washington, D.C., 1970s, Alexander, p. 9; Virginia, 1930s, WPA.

p. 115   *Berries red.* UMA, 1970.

p. 115   *Corn knee-high.* American proverb.

p. 115   *Button to the chin.* Editor's recollection.

p. 116   *Slippy.* See *Showery* below.

p. 116   *The north wind.* Traditional weather rhyme.

p. 116   *Snow, snow faster.* I: Edwin Knowlton, Stonington, Me., 1975.

p. 116   *Showery.* From a seasonal weather rhyme:

> Spring is showery, flowery, bowery,
> Summer is hoppy, croppy, poppy,
> Autumn is wheezy, sneezy, freezy,
> Winter is slippy, drippy, nippy.

13. A TREE

p. 119   *And the green grass.* Widespread camp song, with numerous variants.

14. ANIMALS AND INSECTS

p. 123   *The elephants.* See citation below, p. 126.

p. 124   *Did you ever.* I: Marsha Valance, childhood recollection, Chicago, 1950s.

p. 124   *I have a dog.* Connecticut, 1937, WPA.

p. 125   *I have a dog thin as.* Austin, Tex., 1970, UTA.

p. 125 *Some people say.* Quoted in Loomis, "Mary," p. 47, from *Life* 46 (1905), p. 470.

p. 125 *Mary had a swarm.* I: George R. Huston, Jr., 1948, quoted in Loomis, "Mary," p. 47.

p. 126 *The elephants.* Ten Mile River Boy Scout Camp, Narrowsburg, N.Y., 1940.

p. 128 *On a mule we find.* Oklahoma, 1930s, WPA.

p. 128 *This little mule.* I: F. R. Rubel, Mississippi, 1909, Perrow, p. 125.

p. 128 *The hyena.* Spaeth, p. 76. Adapted.

p. 129 *Panthers scream.* Oklahoma square-dance verse, 1930s, WPA.

p. 129 *The night was dark.* Texas square-dance verse from "It Ain't Gonna Rain No More," UTA.

p. 129 *Birdie, birdie.* Hand-clapping rhyme. I: Jan Derrick, age 10, Hitchcock, Tex., 1968, UTA. English variant from Opie, *Lore*, p. 94:

> When I sat under the apple tree
> A birdie sent his love to me
> And as I wiped it from my eye
> I said "Thank goodness cows can't fly."

p. 130 *The firefly is a funny bird.* New York City, 1930s, WPA.

p. 130 *Oh, say, can you see.* Widespread use. In Austin, Texas, the stew is a barbecue, UTA.

p. 131 *The ants.* Widespread use. One of a family of chain songs including "The Elephants," above; "The Hole in the Bottom of the Sea," and "The Bedbug Song," which starts:

> There were ten in the bed,
> And the little one said,
> "Roll over, roll over"
> So they all rolled over and one fell out,
> And the little one said . . .

St. Clair Shores, Mich., 1980, WSUA.

p. 134 *Be kind.* Widespread use.

15. OTHER THINGS

p. 136   *As wet as a fish.* From a list of rhyming similes, *The Golden Era,* July, 1869, as quoted in "List," pp. 174–5. For other lists, see Loomis, "Rhymed," pp. 282–5; Halpert, pp. 196–7.

p. 136   *Are you a camel.* I: Carol Waldman, Philadelphia, 1964, UPA.

p. 137   *Let me call you.* I: Natalie P. Gordon, Philadelphia, 1964, UPA.

p. 138   *Don't steal this book.* DeKalb, Ill., 1936, WPA.

p. 138   *We are the boys.* New York City, 1938, WPA.

p. 139   *1, 2, 3, 4, 5, 6, 7.* One of many rhymes in this pattern. An Oklahoma variant ends: "7, 6, 5, 4, 3, 2, 1/ All bad children had better run."

p. 139   *Old man Moses.* Colonial Heights School, Stockton, Cal., 1979.

p. 139   *Hiccup, snickup.* I: William Knowlton, Stonington, Me., 1975.

p. 140   *Little seed.* I: Mary Ellen Rogers, Dallas, Tex., 1960s, UTA.

p. 140   *No matter how young.* I: Mary Ellen Rogers, Dallas, Tex., 1960s, UTA.

p. 141   *Open your mouth and close your eyes.* Widespread rhymes used in making a gift of sweets. Popular in late nineteenth, early twentieth centuries.

p. 141   *Under this sod.* Johnston, Colo., 1939, WPA.

p. 142   *Sound the bell!* Mobile, Ala., 1930s, WPA.

p. 143   *When a big tree.* Bloomington, Ind., 1968, IUA.

p. 143   *Often we are foolish.* Austin, Tex., n.d., UTA. Adapted slightly.

p. 144   *Oh, dear, bread and beer.* New England rhyme for a boring visit, Johnson, p. 196.

p. 143   *I'm a little teapot.* Hamilton School, Detroit, 1957, WSUA.

p. 143   *Don't worry.* I: Frankie Ferrar, Chicago, 1953, IUA.

p. 144   *A chicken.* Traditional spelling rhyme.

p. 144   *A knife.* Traditional spelling rhyme.

p. 144   *There was an old man.* Editor's recollection, Northwestern University, Evanston, Ill., 1950s.

p. 145 *Daniel was a naughty man.* Colonial Heights School, Stockton, Cal., 1979.

p. 145 *My mother is a Russian.* New Brunswick, N.J., 1973, RU. During World War II, "my mother" was a German.

p. 145 *Little Miss Muffet.* Editor's recollection.

p. 145 *Ladybug, ladybug.* A traditional rhyme in English-speaking countries, Western Europe, and elsewhere. In England the ladybug of the American rhyme is a "ladybird," the frying pan a "warming pan." A German theory suggests that a similar rhyme was used as a charm to protect the sun as it moved through the redness of the evening sky at sunset, which is represented by the house on fire. Opie, *Dictionary*, pp. 263–64.

p. 146 *I swapped me a horse.* Adapted from several versions, including those in Perrow, p. 143; Sharp, pp. 306–308; Janson, "Note," p. 56; "Further," pp. 87–88; Opie, *Dictionary*, pp. 162–66. The song is best known in America as "The Swapping Song." It may have roots in a fourteenth-century political song from the days of England's King Richard II.

p. 148 *Good night.* Widespread use.

Bibliography

BOOKS

Books that may be of interest to young people are marked with an asterisk (*).

*Abrahams, Roger D., ed. *Jump-Rope Rhymes: A Dictionary.* Austin, Tex.: University of Texas Press, 1969.

*———— and Lois Rankin, eds. *Counting-Out Rhymes: A Dictionary.* Austin, Tex.: University of Texas Press, 1980.

Alexander, Jean. *Jump, Clap and Sing.* Children's Area Festival of American Folklore. Collected from Washington, D.C., Children, 1974.

*Baring-Gould, William S., and Ceil Baring-Gould, eds. *The Annotated Mother Goose: Nursery Rhymes Old and New, Arranged and Explained.* New York: Clarkson N. Potter, Inc., 1962.

Bennett, Charles H., ed. *Old Nurse's Book of Rhymes, Jingles, and Ditties.* London: Griffin and Farran, 1865.

Bolton, Henry C. *The Counting-Out Rhymes of Children.* London: Elliot Stock, 1888. Reprint edition, Detroit: Singing Tree Press, 1969.

Botkin, B. A., ed. *A Treasury of American Folklore.* New York: Crown Publishers, Inc., 1944.

Brewster, Paul G., ed. "Children's Games and Rhymes." In *The Frank C. Brown Collection of North Carolina Folklore*, Vol. 1. Durham, N.C.: Duke University Press, 1952.

*Chase, Richard, ed. *American Folk Tales and Songs.* New York: New American Library of World Literature, 1956. Reprint edition, New York: Dover Publications, 1971.

*Daiken, Leslie, ed. *Children's Games throughout the Year.* London: P. T. Batsford, 1949.

*———. *Out She Goes.* Dublin: The Dolman Press, 1963.

Dorson, Richard. *Buying the Wind: Regional Folklore in the United States.* Chicago: University of Chicago Press, 1964.

*Emrich, Duncan. *The Nonsense Book of Riddles, Rhymes, Tongue Twisters, Puzzles and Jokes from American Folklore.* New York: Four Winds Press, 1970.

Esar, Evan. *The Humor of Humor.* New York: Horizon Press, 1952.

*Evans, Patricia. *Rimbles: A Book of Children's Classic Games, Rhymes, Songs and Sayings.* Garden City, N.Y.: Doubleday & Co., 1961.

Farb, Peter. *Word Play: What Happens When People Talk.* New York: Alfred A. Knopf, Inc., 1974.

*Fowke, Edith F., ed. *Ring Around the Moon.* Englewood Cliffs, N.J.: Prentice-Hall, Inc., 1977.

*———. *Sally Go Round the Sun.* Toronto: McClelland and Stewart, Ltd., 1969.

Halliwell-Phillips, James O. *The Nursery Rhymes of England.* London: Warne & Company, 1842. Reprint edition, London: Bodley Head, 1970.

Hand, Wayland D., ed. "Popular Beliefs and Superstitions." In *The Frank C. Brown Collection of North Carolina Folklore*, Vols. 6, 7. Durham, N.C.: Duke University Press, 1961.

Hand, Wayland D. et al., eds. *Popular Beliefs and Superstitions: A Compendium of American Folklore*, Vols. 1, 2. Boston: G. K. Hall and Company, 1981. (Ohio beliefs.)

Howard, Dorothy Mills. *Folk Jingles of American Children: A Collection and Study of Rhymes Used by Children Today.* Ph.D. dissertation, New York University, 1938.

Johnson, Clifton. *What They Say in New England and Other American Folklore.* Boston: Lee and Shepherd, 1896. Reprint edition, New York: Columbia University Press, 1963.

Knapp, Mary, and Herbert Knapp. *One Potato, Two Potato: The Secret Language of American Children.* New York: W. W. Norton & Company, 1976.

Lomax, John, and Alan Lomax. *American Ballads and Folk Songs*. New York: The Macmillan Company, 1934.

MacThomáis, Éamon. *Janey Mack, Me Shirt Is Black*. Dublin: The O'Brien Press, 1982.

*Morrison, Lillian. *Touch Blue*. New York: Thomas Y. Crowell Company, 1958.

Newell, William W. *Games and Songs of American Children*, 2d ed. New York: Harper and Brothers, 1903. Reprint edition, New York: Dover Publications, 1963.

Opie, Iona, and Peter Opie. *A Family Book of Nursery Rhymes*. New York: Oxford University Press, 1969.

———. *I Saw Esau*. London: Williams and Northgate, 1947.

———. *The Lore and Language of Schoolchildren*. London: Oxford University Press, 1959.

———. *The Oxford Dictionary of Nursery Rhymes*. Oxford: Oxford University Press, 1951.

Puzzledom, An Original Collection of Characters, Conundrums, etc. Philadelphia: William P. Hazard, 1854.

Randolph, Vance, ed. *Ozark Folk Songs*, Vol. 3, "Humorous and Play-Party Songs." Columbia, Missouri: The State Historical Society of Missouri, 1949.

———. *Ozark Superstitions*. New York: Columbia University Press, 1947. Reprint edition, *Ozark Magic and Folklore,* New York: Dover Publications, 1964.

*Ritchie, James R. T. *The Singing Street*. Edinburgh: Oliver and Boyd, 1964.

*Rutherford, Frank. *All the Way to Pennywell: Children's Rhymes of the North East.* Durham, England: University of Durham Institute of Education, 1971.

Sandburg, Carl. *The American Songbag*. New York: Harcourt, Brace and Company, 1927.

*Schwartz, Alvin. *Cross Your Fingers, Spit in Your Hat: Superstitions and Other Beliefs.* Philadelphia and New York: J. B. Lippincott Company, 1974.

*———. *Flapdoodle: Pure Nonsense from American Folklore.* New York: J. B. Lippincott Company, 1980.

*———. *Tomfoolery: Trickery and Foolery With Words.* Philadelphia and New York: J. B. Lippincott Company, 1972.

*———. *Unriddling: All Sorts of Riddles to Puzzle Your Guessery.* New York: J. B. Lippincott, 1983.

*———. *When I Grew Up Long Ago.* Philadelphia and New York: J. B. Lippincott Company, 1978.

Sharp, Cecil J., and Maude Karpeles. *English Folk Songs from the Southern Appalachians,* Vol. 2. New York and London: Oxford University Press, 1932.

Spaeth, Sigmund. *Read 'Em and Weep.* New York: Doubleday, Page & Co., 1927.

Stewart, Susan. *Nonsense: Aspects of Intertextuality in Folklore and Literature.* Baltimore: Johns Hopkins University Press, 1978.

Sutton-Smith, Brian. *The Games of New Zealand Children.* Berkeley, Cal.: University of California Press, 1959.

Talley, Thomas W. *Negro Folk Rhymes, Wise and Otherwise, with a Study.* New York: The Macmillan Company, 1922.

Taylor, Archer. *English Riddles from the Oral Tradition.* Berkeley, Cal.: University of California Press, 1951.

Turner, Ian. *Cinderella Dressed in Yella: The Play-Rhymes of Australian Children.* New York: Taplinger Publishing Company, 1972.

Whitney, Annie W., and Caroline C. Bullock. *Folklore from Maryland. MAFS*, Vol. 18. New York: American Folklore Society, 1925.

*Withers, Carl A. *I Saw a Rocket Walk a Mile: Nonsense Tales, Chants, and Songs from Many Lands.* New York: Holt, Rinehart and Winston, 1965.

*———. *A Rocket in My Pocket: The Rhymes and Chants of Young Americans.* New York: Henry Holt and Company, 1948.

*Wood, Ray. *The American Mother Goose.* Philadelphia and New York: J. B. Lippincott Company, 1938.

*———. *Fun in American Folk Rhymes.* Philadelphia and New York: J. B. Lippincott Company, 1952.

ARTICLES

Abrahams, Roger D. "Circular Jingles." *WF* 17 (1962): 192–94.

Ainsworth, Katherine H. "Jump Rope Verses Around the United States." *WF* 20 (1961): 179–99.

Atkinson, Robert M. "Songs Little Girls Sing: An Orderly Invitation to Violence." *NWF* 2 (1967): 2–8.

Babcock, W. H. "Games of Washington Children." *AA*, old series (1888): 243–84.

Baldwin, Karen. "Rhyming Pieces and Piecin' Rhymes: Recitation Verse and Family Poem-Making." *SFQ* 40 (1976): 209–42.

Bergen, Fanny D., and William W. Newell. "Current Superstitions." *JAF* 2 (1889): 105–12.

Brendle, Thomas R., and William S. Troxell. "Pennsylvania German Songs." In *Pennsylvania Songs and Legends*, George Korson, ed. Philadelphia: University of Pennsylvania Press, 1949. Reprint edition, Baltimore: Johns Hopkins University Press, 1960.

Brewster, Paul G. "The Friendship Verse, a Hardy Perennial." *HF* 5 (1946): 111–14.

Britt, Stewart H., and Margaret M. Balcom. "Jumping-Rope Rhymes and the Social Psychology of Play." *Journal of Genetic Psychology* 58 (1941): 289–306.

Browne, Ray B. "Children's Taunts, Teases and Disrespectful Sayings from Southern California." *WF* 13 (1954): 190–98.

———. "Southern California Jump-Rope Rhymes: A Study in Variants." *WF* 14 (1955): 3–21.

Burling, Robbins. "The Metrics of Children's Verse: A Cross Linguistic Study." *AA* 68 (1966): 1418–41.

Butler, Francelia. "The Poetry of Rope-Skipping: Over the Garden Wall/I Let the Baby Fall . . ." *The New York Times Magazine*, Dec. 16, 1973: 90–95.

Catagna, Barbara. "Some Rhymes, Games, and Songs from Children in the New Rochelle Area." *NYFQ* 25 (1969): 221–36.

Clair, Mimi. "Some Rope-Jumping Rhymes from Berkeley." *WF* 13 (1954): 278–80.

———. "Songs of My Childhood." *WF* 18 (1959): 245–50.

"Counting-Out Verses." *Word-Lore* (1926): 224–26.

Culin, Stewart. "Street Games of Boys in Brooklyn, N.Y." *JAF* 4 (1891): 221–37.

Delaney's Recitations, No. 8. New York: William W. Delaney, n.d.

Dobie, Bertha McKee. "Tales and Rhymes of a Texas Household." PTFS 6 (1927): 23–71.

Dundes, Alan. "Some Minor Genres of American Folklore." *SFQ* 31 (1967): 20–36.

Emrich, Duncan. "Autograph Book Rhymes," prepared for Folk Song Section, Library of Congress, n.d.

Ford, Nancy K. "A Garland of Playground Jingles." *KFQ* 2 (1957–58): 109–11.

Goldstein, Kenneth S. "Strategy in Counting Out: An Ethnographic Folklore Field Study." In *The Study of Games*, Elliott M. Avedon and Brian Sutton-Smith, eds. New York: John Wiley & Sons, 1971.

Halpert, Herbert. "Rhymed Proverbial Comparisons." *WF* 15 (1956): 196–97.

Heck, Jean O. "Folk Poetry and Folk Criticism." *JAF* 40 (1927): 1–77.

Henry, Mellinger E. "Nursery Rhymes and Game Songs from Georgia." *JAF* 47 (1934): 334–40.

Howard, Dorothy Mills. "The Rhythms of Ball-Bouncing and Ball-Bouncing Rhymes." *JAF* 62 (1949): 166–172.

———, and Morris Bishop. "Songs of Innocence." *The New Yorker*, Nov. 13, 1937, pp. 32–36, 42.

"Icka Backa, Soda Cracker." *Time*, May 29, 1950, pp. 19–20.

Janson, William Hugh. "A Further Note on the Swapping Song." *HF* 4 (1945): 87–89.

———. "A Note and a Query." *HF* 4 (1945): 56.

Krueger, John R. "Parodies in the Folklore of a Third-Grader." *SFQ* 32 (1968): 66–68.

Leventhal, Nancy C. and Ed Cray. "Depth Collecting from a Sixth-Grade Class," Part Two. *WF* 22 (1963): 231–57.

"A List of Similes." *WF* 15 (1956): 174–75.

Loomis, C. Grant. "Mary Had a Parody: A Rhyme of Childhood in Folk Tradition." *WF* 17 (1958): 45–51.

———. "Rhymed Proverbial Comparisons." *WF* 14 (1955): 282–85.

Maryott, Florence. "Nebraska Counting-Out Rhymes." *SFQ* 1 (1937): 39–62.

Millard, Eugenia L. "You're It in New York State." *NYFQ* 16 (1960): 145–49.

Monteiro, George. "Parodies of Scripture, Prayer, and Hymn." *JAF* 77 (1964): 43–52.

Musick, Ruth Ann, and Vance Randolph. "Children's Rhymes from Missouri." *JAF* 63 (1950): 425–37.

Nulton, Lucy. "Jump Rope Rhymes as Folk Literature." *JAF* 61 (1948): 53–67.

Paredes, Americo. "Some Aspects of Folk Poetry." *TSLL* 6 (1964–65): 213–25.

Perrow, E. C. "Songs and Rhymes from the South." *JAF* 26 (1913): 123–73.

Porter, Kenneth. "Circular Jingles and Repetitious Rhymes." *WF* 17 (1958): 107–11.

Randolph, Vance. "Jump Rope Rhymes from Arkansas." *MF* 3 (1953): 77–84.

———, and May K. McCord. "Autograph Albums in the Ozarks." *JAF* 61 (1948): 182–91.

Reck, Alma K. "Skip and Sing!" *WF* 8 (1949): 126–30.

Stimson, Anna K. "Cries of Defiance and Derision, and Rhythmic Chants of West Side New York City, 1893–1903." *JAF* 56 (1945): 124–29.

Story, M. L. "The Folk-Lore of Adolescence: Autograph Books." *SFQ* 17 (1953): 207–12.

Sutton-Smith, Brian. "The Games of Children." In *Our Living Tradition: An Introduction to American Folklore,* Tristram P. Coffin, ed. New York: Basic Books, 1948.

Waugh, F. W. "Canadian Folk-Lore from Ontario." *JAF* 31 (1918): 4–82.

Weaver, Linda. "Camp Songs: Reflection of Youth." *NCFJ* 22 (1974): 75–79.

Winslow, David J. "Children's Derogatory Epithets." *JAF* 82 (1969): 255–63.

———. "An Annotated Collection of Children's Lore." *KFQ* 11 (1966): 151–207.

Woodward, Robert H. "Folklore Marginalia in Old Textbooks." *NYFQ* 18 (1962): 24–27.

Yoffie, Leah R.C. "Three Generations of Children's Singing Songs in St. Louis." *JAF* 60 (1947): 25–51.

Index of First Lines

Fat, fat, the water rat, 35
Feed it, it will grow high, 88
First a daughter, then a son, 2
Flies forever, rests never, 89
Fortune-teller, fortune-teller, 45
Four stiff-standers, 85
Fudge, fudge, tell the judge, 2

Gene, Gene, made a machine, 12
Gilly, gilly, gilly, gilly, 108
Good night, sleep tight, 148

Hark, the herald angels shout, 32
He is handsome, he is pretty, 48
Heigh-ho, heigh-ho, I bit the
    teacher's toe, 29
Heigh-ho, heigh-ho, it's off to
    school we go, 26
Here comes teacher, and she is
    yellin', 26
Here comes teacher with a great
    big stick, 26
Here comes the bride, 55
Here I stand all fat and
    chunky, 15
Hiccup, snickup, 139
Higglety, pigglety, pop, 74

I ain't been to Frisco, 102
I eat my peas with honey, 20
I have a dog, his name is
    Rover, 124
I have a dog thin as a rail, 125
I love that black-eyed boy, 51
I love you, I love you, I love you, I
    do, 37
I love you, I love you, I love you
    lots, 53

I never saw such eyes as thine, 49
I saw a peacock with a fiery
    tail, 90
I scream, you scream, 23
I swapped me a horse and got me
    a cow, 146
I was my mother's darling
    child, 2
I went downtown, 99
I win one game, 105
I wish I had a nickel, 50
I wish I were a dancer, 46
I wish my mother would hold her
    tongue, 51
I wish you luck, 56
I with I wath a fith, 10
I would reduce, 8
If I had you for a
    teacher, 32
If your nose itches, 42
If your shoelace comes
    untied, 42
I'm a pretty little Dutch girl, 103
I'm a little teapot stout, 143
I'm the boss, Applesauce, 37
I'm up here in the nuthouse, 80
In the beginning I seem
    mysterious, 91
In the woods there was a
    hole, 119
Intie, mintie, tootsie, lala, 94
It runs all day, but never
    walks, 89
It stays all year, 89
It's raining, it's
    pouring, 113
I've been working on my
    schoolbooks, 27

An Acknowledgment

For their generous help, I thank the hundreds of young people, librarians and teachers who shared their rhymes and songs with me.

I also thank the archivists at the following folklore archives for helping in my search for folk poetry from earlier generations: Wayne State University; the University of Pennsylvania; Indiana University; the Northeast Archives of Folklore and Oral History; University of Maine, Orono; the Barker Texas History Center; University of Texas, Austin; and the Library of Congress.

I also acknowledge my considerable debt to the scholars who have gathered, preserved and studied our folk poetry.

I also am grateful to Edward Ives, Joseph Hickerson, Gerald Parsons, Kenneth Goldstein, Janet Langlois, Dudley Carlson, and John Wheat for their many courtesies and to Barbara Carmer Schwartz for her great help.

A. S.